TECHNOLOGY AND SOCIETY IN THE MEDIEVAL CENTURIES:
BYZANTIUM, ISLAM, AND THE WEST, 500–1300

AMERICAN HISTORICAL ASSOCIATION–
SOCIETY FOR THE HISTORY OF TECHNOLOGY

HISTORICAL PERSPECTIVES ON TECHNOLOGY, SOCIETY, AND CULTURE

A SERIES EDITED BY PAMELA O. LONG AND ROBERT C. POST

TECHNOLOGY AND SOCIETY IN THE MEDIEVAL CENTURIES: BYZANTIUM, ISLAM, AND THE WEST, 500–1300

BY PAMELA O. LONG

A PUBLICATION OF THE SOCIETY FOR THE HISTORY OF TECHNOLOGY AND THE AMERICAN HISTORICAL ASSOCIATION

Pamela O. Long is an independent historian who has published extensively on medieval and late medieval/Renaissance cultural history, history of science, and technology. Her fellowships have included a Folger Shakespeare Library NEH long-term fellowship (1994–95), a senior fellowship at the Dibner Institute for the History of Science and Technology at the Massachusetts Institue of Technology (2000–01), the Andrew W. Mellon Foundation Post-Doctoral Rome Prize Fellowship from the American Academy in Rome (2003–04), and grants from the National Science Foundation. Her publications include *Openness, Secrecy, Authorship: Technical Arts and the Culture of Knowledge from Antiquity to the Renaissance* (Baltimore, Md.: Johns Hopkins University Press, 2001), awarded the Morris D. Forkosch Prize by the *Journal of the History of Ideas* for the best first book in intellectual history published in 2001, and one of the previous booklets in the AHA/SHOT series—*Technology, Society, and Culture in Late Medieval/Renaissance Europe, 1300–1600*.

Cover Illustration: *Building the Tower of Babel.* Drawing from Herrad of Landsberg, Hortus deliciarum, twelfth century (original destroyed). Equipment seen here includes a hoe, at left; a hod (second figure from left) for carrying mortar; a pick, chisel, and mallet used by the stone-cutters on the right; a plumbline held by the man on the top; and a mason's trowel and mason's square held by the man standing at right-center. From *Das Lustgärtlein der Herrad von Landsberg*, ed. Maria Heinsius (Kolmar im Elass: Alsatia Verlag, n.d.), plate 7.

Author's Note: For the sake of simplicity I have avoided special characters in Arabic words and used the Gregorian calendar rather than the lunar calendar used by Muslims. I would like to warmly thank the readers of the manuscript who have saved me from many infelicities and errors—Glenn Bugh, Thomas F. Glick, Bert S. Hall, Richard W. Bulliet, and Steven A. Walton. I also thank Bob Post for heroic editing and Bob Korn for creating the maps and for extensive assistance with the illustrations. Any remaining errors are my own.

Layout: Christian A. Hale

This booklet series is published with financial assistance from the Dibner Fund, Inc.

© 2003 American Historical Association

Published in 2003 by the American Historical Association. As publisher, the American Historical Association does not adopt official views on any field of history and does not necessarily agree or disagree with the views expressed in this book.

Library of Congress Cataloging-in-Publication data:
Long, Pamela O.
   Technology and society in the medieval centuries: Byzantium, Islam, and the West, 500–1300 / Pamela O. Long.
   p. cm. -- (Historical perspectives on technology, society, and culture)
   ISBN 0-87229-132-4
   1. Technology--Social aspects--Byzantine Empire--History. 2.Technology--Social aspects--Islamic Empire--History. 3.Technology--Social aspects--Europe--History. 4. Civilization,Medieval. I. Title. II. Series.
T14.5.L66 2003
303.48'3'0902--dc22   2003015953

TABLE OF CONTENTS

SERIES INTRODUCTION

Technology reflects and shapes human history. From hunting and gathering cultures and the establishment of neolithic villages, farming, and food storage techniques to the development of metallurgy, ceramics, and weaving; firearms, printing, and mechanized power; and automation, electronics, and computers, history and technology have been integral with one another. The role and function of specific technologies—flint tools in the paleolithic and pottery in the neolithic, the stirrup in the Middle Ages, gunpowder and the mechanical clock in the thirteenth century, printing presses in the fifteenth and sixteenth, the steam engine in the eighteenth, factories in the nineteenth, and the automobile and nuclear power in the twentieth—are all subjects of an expansive scholarly literature. Throughout this literature are animated controversies concerning the choices made among competing techniques for attaining the same end—whether automobiles would be powered by steam, electricity, or internal combustion, for example, or whether computers would be analog or digital.

Yet for all its importance, technology and its mutual interactions with society and culture are rarely addressed in high school, or college, or even in university history courses. When scholars unfamiliar with its rich historiography do consider technology, they typically treat it as inert or determinate, lending their authority to the fallacy that it advances according to its own internal logic. Specialists in the history of technology now recognize the importance of "social construction": technologies succeed or fail (or emerge at all) partly because of the political strategies employed by individual, group, and organizational "actors" who have conflicting or complementary interests in particular outcomes. Many of us believe that success and failure is contingent on inescapable physical realities as well as ambient sociocultural factors. But there is no doubt that technological designs are shaped by such factors; nor, indeed, that the shaping of technology is *integral* to the shaping of society and culture.

This joint venture of the American Historical Association and the Society for the History of Technology draws on the analytical insights of scholars who address technology in social and cultural context, whether their discipline be history or another field in the humanities or social sciences. Authors of these booklets may be concerned with the effects of particular technologies on particular constituencies; with the relationship of technology to labor, economics, and the organization of production; with the role technology plays in differentiating social status and the construction of gender; or with interpretive flexibility—namely, the perception that determinations about whether a technology "works" are contingent on the expectations, needs, and ideology of those who interact with it. Following from this is the understanding that technology is not intrinsically useful or even rational; capitalist ideology in

vii

particular has served to mask powerful nonutilitarian motives for technological novelty, among them kinesthetic pleasure, a sense of play, curiosity, and the exercise of ingenuity for its own sake, a phenomenon known as technological enthusiasm. As evidence of this, many modern inventions—from the telephone to the automobile to new materials such as celluloid and aluminum—met only marginal needs at the outset. Needs with any substantial economic significance often had to be *contrived*, thereby making invention the mother of necessity.

There are many definitions of technology. Often they are ahistorical, particularly those that define technology in terms of applying science to industrial and commercial objectives. Sometimes technology is defined as the way that "things are done or made." While this is not a historian's definition per se, it becomes that whenever one asks how things were done or made in a particular way in a particular context and then analyzes the implications of taking one path rather than another. Lynn White Jr., a historian who served as president of both the Society for the History of Technology and the American Historical Association, called this "the jungle of meaning." While the notion that technology marches of its own predetermined accord still has a strong hold on popular sensibilities, specialists in the interaction of technology and culture now understand that it cannot do anything of the sort. Technology is not autonomous; rather it is impelled by choices made in the context of circumstances in ambient realms, very often in the context of disputes over political power. Once chosen, however, technologies themselves can exert a powerful influence on future choices. One only needs to consider the Strategic Defense Initiative, "Star Wars," which keeps getting funded not because it is actually feasible but because it provides partisans with effective political rhetoric.

To some extent, definitions of technology vary from one discipline to another. We believe that defining it as "the sum of the methods by which a social group provides themselves with the material objects of their civilization" is sufficiently concrete without being too confining and without being misleading. It is important to specify the word *material*, for there are of course "techniques" having to do with everything from poetics to sex to bureaucratic administration. Some might go further and specify that "material" be taken to mean three-dimensional "things," and this seems satisfactory as long as one bears in mind that even an abstraction such as a computer program, or an idea for the design of a machine, or an ideology such as technocracy or scientific management is contingent for expression upon tangible artifacts.

"Technology" is a modern word, dating to the early nineteenth century. Its first well-known usage was in an 1831 treatise by Jacob Bigelow entitled *Elements of Technology*. For some time after that—and maybe even today—it was not a term known to every culture. "Mechanical arts," used in medieval and early modern Europe, is not entirely synonymous, since this term included painting and sculpture as well as machinery, mills, and the like. Technology encompasses various actors' categories in diverse historical cultures, and that is part of the reason why contemporary scholars define it variously. We believe that the complexity of definition, conceptual categories, and methodologies is instrumental in making the history of technology such a fascinating and fruitful area of inquiry. In these booklets, each author may be grounding his or her inquiry on somewhat different assumptions about the nature of the subject matter.

"Every generation writes its own history," said Carl Becker. In commissioning and editing these essays, we have sought to have each one convey a broadly informed synthesis of the best scholarship, to outline the salient historiographical issues, and to highlight interpretive stances that seem persuasive to our own generation. We believe that historians of technology are poised to integrate their inquiries with mainstream scholarship, and we trust that these booklets provide ample confirmation of this belief.

Pamela O. Long
Robert C. Post
Series Editors

INTRODUCTION: THE MEDIEVAL CENTURIES AND THE HISTORY OF TECHNOLOGY

The premise informing this booklet is that technology is embedded in culture, in society, and in the physical environment. This premise underlies an approach to the history of technology in the medieval centuries—and indeed in all times—that emphasizes the rich political, religious, and economic context in which individuals and communities have sought to manipulate their environment, producing crops such as barley and wheat; turning these into foods and beverages such as porridge, bread, and beer; and fabricating material objects for use in agriculture, in the household, and in warfare. They also invented tools, machines, and other devices to which historians of technology have devoted much study. Historians of technology study such inventions, but by no means are they limited to them. Rather, as it is conceived here, technology includes the full range of activities whereby humans manipulate the material world and provide themselves with consumables and materials as well as devices such as plows, weapons, looms, and mills.

This booklet focuses on the medieval centuries between 500 and 1300 and on three contiguous and partially overlapping geopolitical and cultural regions: the Byzantine Empire, the Islamic states, and that part of Europe historians call "the west." The dominant geographic feature of this vast area is the Mediterranean Sea, the "corrupting sea" as it is called in a recent study that investigates the paradox of relatively easy communication among fragmented micro-regions, coastland and islands.[1] Yet the purview of this booklet extends beyond the Mediterranean, eastward to include the regions of Islamic conquest encompassing the Sasanian Empire (present-day Iran and southern Iraq), and northward to include Scandinavia.

In the year 500 C.E., only the Byzantine Empire and the disparate territories of Europe existed as defined entities. The Islamic states existed only in kernel, so to speak, within the future of the settled communities and nomadic tribes of the Arabian Peninsula. Many parts of these regions shared the common heritage of the ancient Roman Empire. Two of them were Christian; Islam emerged in the seventh century as a new monotheistic religion that incorporated earlier Jewish and Christian traditions but added the teachings of the prophet Muhammad (571–632) and the authority of a new holy book, the *Koran*. All three regions subsumed a great variety of peoples, languages, and cultures. The dominant language of Byzantium was Greek and that of the expanding Islamic territories was Arabic, while the official language of the west—the language of the learned—was Latin. Ordinary people in all three regions spoke numerous other languages such as Syriac, Coptic, Hebrew, and the languages of Europe that became the so-called vernaculars.[2]

1

Scholars often treat Byzantium, the Islamic states, and the west separately, both in general histories and within the history of technology. This has the advantage of narrative manageability, but it can lead to serious distortions. While the Byzantine Empire is frequently ignored altogether, the Islamic territories are often treated collectively in histories of medieval technology as a great highway that transmitted inventions originating in China on to the west. This is typically freighted with assumptions about progress being something *peculiarly* western. Although economic historians often take technological progress as a structuring paradigm, in recent years historians of technology have started to question explicit or implicit assumptions about progress. They ask: What exactly is meant by progress? Progress for whom? Is situation A actually comparable to situation B? What are the views of historical actors themselves? What is the historical context of specific inventions and their deployment? How do technologies function within the wider social, religious, and political culture? In what ways are particular technologies in the service of those who wield power?[3] Such questions suggest a concern with the ways in which traditional technologies functioned in discrete historical environments, and an interest in reasons why historical actors adopted particular inventions and used them in particular ways.

Treating the Byzantine Empire, the Islamic states, and the European west together invites and facilitates a comparative approach to the history of technology. The three shared much in common but were marked by important religious and cultural differences as well. Though often in conflict with one another, they also engaged in many forms of exchange. As a result of shifting political and military fortunes, their geographic borders were chronically unstable.

The term Byzantine (which derives from the name of the ancient city of Byzantium) did not come into common usage until the Renaissance. But historians now apply it to the political entity that began with the establishment of the eastern Roman Empire in 324 by the Emperor Constantine—who changed the name of the city Byzantium to Constantinople—and came to an end in 1453 when that capital city was conquered by the Ottoman Turks. During its eleven-century history, the Byzantine Empire encompassed a territory with radically changing boundaries. At its greatest extent during the sixth century, it was bound on the east by the Sasanian (Persian) Empire. To the south and west, the conquests of the Emperor Justinian (527–565) gave the Byzantines control of the Mediterranean Sea as well as Anatolia (the region of present-day Turkey), Syria, Palestine, Egypt, north Africa, Greece, the Adriatic Sea, and parts of Italy and the Iberian Peninsula. (See Map 1 on page 8.) Within a century after Justinian's conquests, however, the Arabs had taken not only the old Sasanian Empire but also Egypt, north Africa, and Spain.[4] (See Map 2 on page 20.)

The so-called Latin west comprised regions of the western Mediterranean, northern Europe, and the British Isles. In the fifth century, Germanic peoples such as the Angles and the Saxons, the Ostrogoths, and the Visigoths occupied many of the western territories. While the Byzantine Empire remained a unified entity, albeit one with shifting boundaries, western European lands were divided into

2

separate kingdoms such as the Kingdom of the Franks in Gaul, of the Visigoths in Spain, and of the Lombards in Italy. The greatest degree of unity in the west was achieved by the emperor Charlemagne (c. 742–814). Charlemagne's military and administrative genius, along with his careful cultivation of a fruitful alliance with the Catholic church, enabled him to rule a vast area of western Europe, what is now known as the Carolingian Empire. (See Map 3 on page 38.) Crowned by the Pope in Rome in the year 800, he became the first "Holy Roman Emperor." But after his death his empire soon broke up into smaller entities.[5]

In the ninth century the peoples of Europe were besieged by Muslims from the Mediterranean, and also besieged from the east by the Magyars (later called Hungarians), and from the north by the Vikings. A group of Vikings who came to be called Normans settled in northwestern France. Eventually one group of Normans conquered Sicily and southern Italy, and then another group led by William the Conqueror (1027–87) conquered Anglo-Saxon England in the Battle of Hastings in 1066. During the tenth and eleventh centuries western Europe gradually became more stable as regional monarchies such as the Anglo-Normans in England and the Capetians in France consolidated their power.[6]

The Islamic states developed after the prophet Muhammad founded the new religion of Islam in the early seventh century. Muhammad preached first in Mecca and then in the oasis town of Medina on the Arabian Peninsula. His initial followers were townsmen and merchants who eventually gained the support of the nomadic tribes who dominated the peninsula. The early Muslims consolidated their power in Arabia and then turned toward the Byzantine Empire, conquering part of it between 633 and 640 and then moving toward the Sasanian Empire to the east, conquering it by 650.[7]

By 642, Arab armies had defeated Byzantine forces in Egypt. After a period of civil war between 656 and 661, conquests continued under the Umayyad caliphs who ruled from Damascus. By 713 the Arabs had reached the Indus Valley in the east, and in the west they had taken control of the Iberian Peninsula by 711. Eventually the Umayyad caliphate lost power to the Abbasid caliphs who ruled from Baghdad starting in 750, but, with the decline of the Abbasids during the next century, the Islamic Empire lost its unity. Egypt was ruled by the Fatimids after 909, while Spain was governed by the Spanish Umayyads after 912. In 1096, there began a long series of western incursions on Byzantine and Islamic lands, incursions called the Crusades. Counterattacks included the notable victories of the Muslims under Saladin (1138–93). During the fourteenth century the Crusaders confronted new adversaries, the Mongols, but that takes us beyond the time frame of this booklet.[8]

The vast geographical reach and the complexity of the medieval world demands a cautious approach in recounting the history of its technologies, a methodology that avoids some of the over-generalizations that have been made in the past. For example, early studies of "manorialism" focused on France, England, and northern German lands. Then the term was applied to the Italian and Iberian peninsulas, but often inappropriately. Similarly, the term "feudalism" has been imbued with vastly different meanings and applied to social and political relationships in widely differing societies. In addition, the history of medieval technology seems to be a magnet for the term "revolution," including supposed agricultural and industrial revolutions in medieval Europe and even an Arab "green revolution." As we shall see, the use of this term to characterize subtle and complex changes in agriculture and technology has been challenged by scholars on a number of fronts. While there is no doubt that the world of 1300 was profoundly different from that of 500, "revolution" suggests a rate of change more rapid than many historians are now willing to accept.

Some of the greatest historians of the twentieth century were medievalists whose work impinged upon and profoundly enriched the historiography of medieval technology. While some of their ideas have now been revised, even rejected, their work has left a permanent impress on the field. The most important of these scholars was the Belgian historian Henri Pirenne (1862–1935). The author of a foundational study on the history of Belgium, Pirenne was imprisoned during the First World War for defying the German invaders. After his release in 1918 he turned to broader themes, developing what has become known as the Pirenne thesis. The most important statement of this thesis appears in a short work, translated as *Mohammed and Charlemagne*, the first draft of which was finished in 1935 shortly before Pirenne's death.[9]

Pirenne was one of the first scholars to think about the relationship between the ancient and medieval worlds. In *Mohammed and Charlemagne* he argued that the Germanic tribes that penetrated the Roman Empire between the fourth and sixth centuries preserved many Roman political institutions as well as urban culture, and that trade in the Mediterranean remained active. He further argued that it was the Islamic conquests of the seventh and early eighth centuries that effectively split the eastern Mediterranean from the west and isolated the Frankish kings in northwest Europe. One result was the rise of the Carolingians, who were not fundamentally oriented to the Mediterranean. For Pirenne, the end of the classical world came in the seventh century with the collapse of the commercial classes of the west and the ascendancy of landholders.[10]

From the time of its publication, the Pirenne thesis has been debated. Scholars who sought to qualify or even refute it have shown that Pirenne underestimated the decline of the Roman Empire even before the Germanic incursions, overestimated the effect of the Islamic expansion on trade, and failed to recognize the importance of regional economies. And yet the long shadow of Pirenne still hovers over medieval studies in ways that are particularly relevant to the study of medieval technology. Because it included assertions about long-distance trade and the status of towns throughout the Mediterranean and Europe, the Pirenne thesis was particularly amenable to testing by means of the evidence presented in material objects. It provided a starting-point for important investigations by scholars in a great variety of disciplines, from numismatics to archaeology.[11]

In recent decades, new methodologies have produced much new data, as a result of digitalized databases of primary sources; prospopography or collective biography and the use of travelers' accounts to trace movements of people and goods; and even DNA studies of medieval remains. The field of medieval archaeology also has expanded and matured. Numerous new dating and identification techniques have been developed. Fieldwork has been transformed with greater concern for regional studies rather than single-site excavations. There have been extensive analyses of settlement patterns, the production of goods, and patterns of distribution. The rise, stability, or decline of particular towns has been studied empirically, as has the circulation of artifacts such as pottery and glass, and the characteristics of particular technologies. The range of empirical data for early medieval history, especially as it concerns many aspects of material culture, has been greatly expanded—much to the benefit of historians of medieval technology.[12]

Henri Pirenne has been called the patron saint of the *Annales* school of historiography that developed in the 1920s. The *Annalists* explicitly rejected an "event-oriented" nationalist history which failed to grasp the richness of human reality. Led by Marc Bloch (1886–1944) and Lucien Febvre (1878–1956), a small group of European historians set out to expand the range of historical studies beyond their traditional focus on war, politics, diplomacy, and great leaders. These historians worked to create stronger analytical frameworks, and to incorporate the insights of sociology and economic history. For the new history, Bloch and Febvre created a new journal, the *Annales d'histoire économique et histoire*, in 1929. Bloch advocated a comparative method drawing on economic and social history, and he considered technology as a fundamental concern along with rural and agrarian history. In a special issue of the *Annales* published in 1935 and devoted to the history of technology, Febvre suggested that the new discipline "incorporate all the uneven, accidental, and human elements of science and invention." Bloch traced the history of waterpower from ancient times through the industrial age, and tied the medieval adoption of the overshot waterwheel to the power of feudal lords on the medieval manor.[13]

Bloch joined the French Resistance and was killed by a German firing squad in 1944. Eighteen years later, the preeminent American historian of medieval technology, Lynn White Jr. (1907–87), dedicated a book to Bloch. This was his widely influential *Medieval Technology and Social Change*. White, whose first scholarship concerned Latin monasticism in Norman Sicily, had turned to the history of technology in response to his concerns about losing access to European archives in the late 1930s during what threatened to be a long European war. Deeply influenced by Bloch's scholarship, especially his work on French rural history, White published numerous studies on subjects that ranged from the role of the stirrup in the development of feudalism to the relationships between medieval religion and technology. Several of his hypotheses—the one concerning the role of the stirrup, for example, and his notion of a medieval agricultural revolution—have been roundly criticized by other historians. Yet his broad interests and the range of his scholarship have insured his continuing influence on the discipline of the history of technology, especially as it concerns the medieval centuries.[14]

5

In the last half of the twentieth century, historians rarely matched the scholarly range of Pirenne, Bloch, or White. Rather, scholarship on medieval technology has focused on the particular—particular places, specific technologies. Such studies have provided a rich trove of empirical data and analysis that can provide a foundation for broader synthetic work. Particularly important is the interdisciplinary cooperation between historians of technology and archaeologists. Recently, ambitious, wide-ranging studies have appeared which combine the virtues of in-depth empirical research and broader historical vision. They include Anna Muthesian's studies of Byzantine silks, Jonathan Bloom's studies of Islamic paper, Peregine Horden and Nicholas Purcell's address to the ancient and medieval Mediterranean, and Michael McCormick's massive and important investigation of the origins of the European economy.[15]

This booklet provides an introduction to recent scholarship and to some of the significant issues in the historiography of medieval technology. In the first part, the first three chapters treat Byzantium, the Islamic lands, and the European west, in that order; these chapters are not strictly parallel, but all three address agriculture, architecture and building, and the crafts. The three chapters in the second part are topical. They treat warfare, travel and transport, and communication, highlighting their interrelationships. No work of history, certainly not a work of this modest size, can hope to treat a subject as vast as this one in a comprehensive manner. What it aims to do, instead, is to open a door to a fascinating and growing discipline—the history of medieval technology—and address technologies as they developed in three contiguous and overlapping cultures. Such an approach encourages thinking about the ways in which these cultures approached similar technological problems in different ways on the basis of differing precepts. At the same time, it seeks to replace a model that contrasts "progress" and "backwardness" with a concern for understanding the ways in which different cultures adopt and transform technologies in ways appropriate to their own needs and their own cultural proclivities.

Map 1. *The Byzantine Empire c. 600.*

1

TECHNOLOGY IN THE BYZANTINE EMPIRE

In the eleven centuries between 324 and 1453, the territorial reach of Byzantium fluctuated radically. As noted in the introduction, the empire attained its maximum extent around 600 C.E. (Map 1), then diminished as a result of Arab conquests. During the late sixth and early seventh centuries, there also occurred massive incursions of Slavic peoples; ultimately the Danube frontier collapsed and the Byzantines lost control of the Balkan peninsula. Later, as western Europe gained ascendancy, the Fourth Crusade (1204) ended with the capture of Constantinople itself. Thereafter, a variety of successor states ruled the empire until finally it was conquered by the Ottoman Turks in 1453.[1]

While the empire thrived, a key characteristic of the Byzantine state was the power of the central government. The emperor and/or empress lived in the splendid imperial palace in Constantinople and presided over an imperial court which controlled an immense civilian bureaucracy. In the early empire, cities governed themselves through city councils or *curia*, made up of large landholders, *decurions*. Members of the *decurion* class were required by the central government to serve on councils responsible for repairing aqueducts, public buildings, and fortifications; cleaning and maintaining the streets; and overseeing the market, tasks for which they often needed to use some of their own resources. As these tasks grew more onerous, they sought to evade them by a variety of means, and ultimately they succeeded. The city councils had virtually disappeared by the mid-sixth century. The gap was filled by provincial governors and, increasingly, by bishops.[2]

AGRICULTURE

The main source of wealth in the Byzantine Empire was agriculture. Crops included wheat, barley, and beans. Flax was used for making linen. In many areas the soil was rocky, water insufficient, summers hot. The Byzantines practiced labor-intensive techniques of dry-farming, including the frequent plowing and hoeing needed to break up the soil and control weeds. They cultivated both winter and summer crops. Winter crops, planted in November, benefited from the Mediterranean's autumn rainfall. Grains and beans constituted an important part of the diet. Kitchen gardens included cabbage, onions, leeks, carrots, garlic, cucumbers, squash, and melons. Vineyards were planted extensively, as were olive trees, even in desert areas such as Syria. Wine was the staple drink of Mediterranean peoples (except the Egyptians, who usually consumed beer), and olive oil was used

9

everywhere in cooking. An abundance of fruit and nut trees included date palms, figs, apples, plums, cherries, almonds, chestnuts, and pistachios. Peasants raised cattle, sheep, goats, and pigs, and used oxen, horses, donkeys, and camels for hauling, plowing, and numerous other tasks.[3]

In addition to large vineyards, peasants often planted a few vines among orchards and gardens. With a pruning knife (*klaudeutērion*), they harvested grapes in bunches and placed them in a large vat, removing leaves and the rotting grapes that would create a bitter taste (Figure 1). After washing their feet, they climbed into the vat and trampled the grapes, extracting the juice which ran into a receptacle. Removing the seeds, they poured the remaining liquid into casks to ferment.[4]

Figure 1. *Noah's sons picking grapes, a detail from the story of The Flood in a Byzantine mosaic of the twelfth century. Cappella Palatina, Palazzo Reale, Palermo, Italy. Note the pruning knife in the right hand of the figure on the left. To make the mosaic, artisans prepared the wall with three layers of plaster. With the first layer, they smoothed irregular surfaces and corners. The second layer served as thinner. They often painted the third layer while the plaster was still wet to match the colors of the tesserae (small pieces of glass, terracotta, or stone), which they set in immediately after the layer was applied. Photo credit: Erich Lessing/Art Resource, New York.*

The production of olive oil was more complicated, involving three different operations. Archaeologists know these processes in part from the excavations of olive mills and oil presses in Syrian sites dating from the fifth through the seventh centuries. Workers dumped the olives into a vat and crushed them (but not the pits) with a stone roller (Figure 2). After removing the dregs, they placed the olive paste in baskets and put these in a second vat, one basket on top of the other. When they lowered a horizontal beam to crush the paste, oil flowed into a vat below. The workers then poured the oil into yet another vat filled with water, so that the impurities settled to the bottom while the oil rose to the top, whence it was drawn off into another container.[5] (See Figure 3.)

Peasants prepared fields for grain cultivation with the *sol ard*, a wooden scratch plow perfectly suited to the dry, rocky soil of much of the empire. It was built with many small variations over time and depending on the location, but always there were four basic parts—the plow beam, yoke beam, stilt, and share beam. (See Figure 4.) The *sol ard* was drawn by oxen harnessed at their necks, urged on by the peasant's goad. As the plowshare was dragged through the top layer of soil, it created a furrow, the depth of which was controlled by pressure on the stilt. With a shallow furrow, moisture was retained in the lower soil. Because the *sol ard* lacked a mold-board to turn the clods over, it was necessary to cross-plow. Where soil was too poor for plowing, peasants tilled manually.[6]

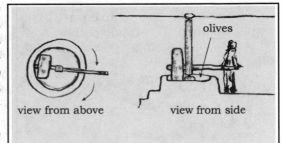

Figure 2. *An olive mill, after Olivier Callot,* **Huileries Antiques de Syrie du Nord** *(Paris: Librairie Orientaliste Paul Geuthner, 1984), plate 123.*

For working soil by hand, there existed a great variety of spades, hoes, and mattocks—a tool resembling a pickaxe. In harvesting grain, peasants held an iron sickle in the right hand and gathered the cut materials with the left. (See Figure 19 on page 42.) They left high stalks and put livestock out to graze it, thereby adding fertilization to the soil. Threshing—the removal of the grain from the stalks—involved spreading sheaves on a threshing floor (often on a hill exposed to winds), where donkeys or oxen would drag a threshing sled (*doukane*) over the sheaves. Peasants then separated grain from chaff with a winnowing fork or shovel. They stored the grain in pits dug in the earth or in the large earthenware vessels called *pithoi* of the sort that are now often found in archaeological excavations.[7]

Most peasants lived in villages. A typical village might include common lands, pastures and forests, a lake or seashore, a spring, vineyards, and groves of olive, walnut, and chestnut trees. Land was often divided into small parcels, and even a large estate might comprise parcels interspersed with other parcels belonging to other estates. Labor was characteristically determined by gender. Women ran the household. They bore and raised children. They cleaned and laundered. They prepared food from scratch, sometimes grinding grain for bread. They made

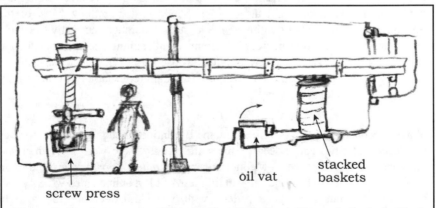

Figure 3. *An oil press, after Olivier Callot,* **Huileries Antiques de Syrie du Nord** *(Paris: Librairie Orientaliste Paul Geuthner, 1984), plate 123.*

11

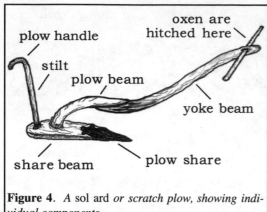

Figure 4. *A sol ard or scratch plow, showing individual components.*

cosmetics and ointments. They attended to all stages of cloth production and the fabrication of garments, from carding wool to spinning, weaving, and sewing. And they worked in the garden and vineyard.[8]

Although peasant families might cultivate their own land, the village as a whole constituted a fiscal and administrative entity, one that was subject to taxation by the central government. Fiscal surveys reveal wide discrepancies in the wealth of villagers, from the landowner who paid a proportionately lower tax to the poorest peasant. There might also be slaves in a village, though there were many more slaves in cities and towns than in the countryside. Power and authority were wielded by hereditary village landowners or by officials of the state bureaucracy such as a tax collector, governor, or judge. The demands of the ubiquitous tax collector often forced peasants to borrow money at high interest rates. Frequently they lost their land because of their inability to repay. A tenant farmer often became tied to the land, his condition hereditary. The lord not only taxed him, he could even chain him if he tried to run away.[9]

Byzantium's great time-span, the paucity of evidence, and the difficulty of interpreting such evidence as does exist all render generalizations about agriculture and the position of peasants difficult and tenuous. Consider the debates surrounding an intriguing document known as the Farmer's Law, eighty-five regulations found in numerous manuscripts after the tenth century. Scholars have dated it variously from the seventh century to the ninth, and have placed it in Italy, in Constantinople, and within the orbit of Slavic customary law. Most of the regulations concern relations within a village, such as damage caused by livestock, theft or trespassing, and sharecropping arrangements among social and economic equals. But, even though the law provides a fascinating view of village life, it cannot be used to generalize about Byzantine agriculture because of the ambiguity concerning its context of origin.[10]

CITIES

While its economic base was agriculture, the Byzantines thought of their empire as a collection of cities and indeed by the sixth century there were more than 900 cities and towns in the eastern Mediterranean. The *polis* or *civitas* consisted of an urban area and the countryside surrounding it. Most Byzantine cities were walled. They were laid out in a regular pattern, with two wide streets meeting at right angles in the center and lined with colonnades under which merchants and artisans sold their goods. Cities usually contained a forum with civic and religious buildings including baths and a basilica—a large rectangular building used for civic and judicial purposes. They also encompassed granaries, aqueducts, and/or cisterns (large basins for collecting rainwater), and they were embellished with statues, fountains, and paintings.[11]

A treatise written in the early 530s by an architect, Julian of Ascalon, provides a glimpse into the life of a Byzantine city during the rule of Justinian I. Ascalon was situated on the Mediterranean coast of Palestine. The treatise promulgated building regulations meant to protect dwellings from damage from nearby construction or other disruptive activities. The architectural historian Besim S. Hakim suggests that the highly prescriptive nature of these regulations "should be viewed in the light of the centralized structure of the Byzantine government in the region." Activities involving fire, smoke, foul odors, and vibrations were regulated. Baths, pottery kilns, kilns for burning lime, bakeries, glass-making workshops, and blacksmith shops all had to be situated at specific distances from existing structures. Workers who pulverized gypsum for use in mortar were required to distance themselves from walls in order to avoid damage. Marinade, in which fish, meat, and vegetables are steeped before cooking, was to be prepared at a distance from dwellings, because it gave off an acrid odor. Rope-makers and fullers (who cleansed and thickened cloth by special processes) were required to have isolated workshops, especially if they burned sulfur. Tavern-keepers were prohibited from putting out benches or straw mattresses for their patrons, or troughs for animals. Brothels were forbidden in cities, although they might be allowed to remain in some villages. Other regulations prohibited construction projects that would block views of the sea, or of the mountains, or even of paintings on the walls of buildings. Not least, strict rules were set down for designing latrines, draining wastewater, and building cisterns.[12]

Byzantine cities experienced many vicissitudes. Population declined radically during the sixth and seventh centuries, a result of plague (which began in 542 and returned periodically until 767), as well as war, conquest, earthquakes, and other catastrophes. During the seventh century, the Byzantines lost much territory to the Arabs and the Slavs, and the effects were devastating, especially since support for the army and administration came from taxing the provinces. As a result, public services were terminated and great public buildings fell into ruin, becoming in effect quarries that provided stones for constructing more modest buildings. As aqueducts were broken, cisterns had to be built everywhere. Great landlords and church officials took over the functions of the defunct city councils. But in 717–18 the Byzantines defended Constantinople from the last Arab siege and after that Byzantine fortunes turned. Between the ninth and twelfth centuries there was considerable urban recovery. Through it all, Constantinople continued to function as the capital and commercial center of the empire.[13]

Constantine I had founded Constantinople in 324, on the site of the Greek city of Byzantion. He and successive Roman emperors erected palaces, the hippodrome, and governmental buildings; wide colonnaded streets, public baths, theaters, churches, and forums; and encompassing sets of walls and the "golden gate" in the form of a triumphal arch. During the Nika revolt of 532, a mutiny provoked by the severe fiscal policies of Emperor Justinian I (527–65) and the extortions of his officials, rioters burned the center of the city, including the church, *Hagia Sophia* (meaning "Holy Wisdom"). In crushing the revolt, Justinian killed at least 30,000 people, according to the Byzantine historian Procopius. Then he began a great building program that transformed the heart of the city. He also constructed churches and fortifications in other parts of the Empire.[14]

ARCHITECTURE AND BUILDING CONSTRUCTION

The most remarkable result of Justinian's building program was the great cathedral of Constantinople, the new *Hagia Sophia*—the largest domed building in the world for centuries thereafter. (See Figure 5.) The architects combined traditional Roman methods with innovative techniques of their own. Built with astounding rapidity between 532 and 537, *Hagia Sophia* comprised a huge square hall covered by a massive hemispherical dome made of bricks set in mortar. The dome rests on four piers from which spring pendentives—that is, spandrels in the form of spherical triangles that form the transition between the piers and the dome. The hall is separated into three aisles by rows of columns. Galleries are situated over the lateral aisles and over the transverse vestibule at the entrance, called the narthex. The eight main piers are built of large blocks of ashlar, squared blocks of building stone. The walls are made with thin bricks set in 2-1/2-inch mortar beds, interspersed with courses of limestone. Such brickwork formed notably light, thin vaults.[15]

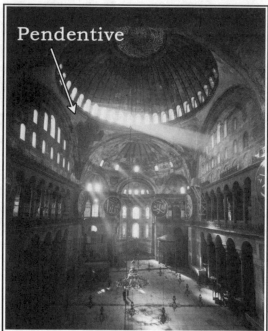

Figure 5. *Interior of* Hagia Sophia, Istanbul, Turkey. *The pendentive is the concave spandrel between the base of the circular dome and the angle of the two walls, allowing the dome to be supported by a square component of the building. Photo credit: Erich Lessing/Art Resource, New York.*

The Great Church, as it was called, was a remarkable engineering feat, and remains so to this day. Windows surrounding the base of the dome make it appear to be suspended above the vast interior space. Robert Mark's structural modeling of the building, using modern techniques of stress analysis, has shown that these windows serve a

14

structural function by preventing cracking, a process to which Roman concrete domes such as the Pantheon were quite vulnerable. Even without the tools of modern stress analysis, Byzantine architects would have observed cracks in existing domes; in the windows of *Hagia Sophia*, they provided a solution to the problem. The Great Church is a complex structure that also has a complex history, including partial collapses and reconstructions, the first in 556. Yet, the building one sees today is still fundamentally the same one built by Justinian's architects—who, as Rowland J. Mainstone put it, "created an immense interior of wide-spanning vaults and subtly interpenetrating spaces that has never been surpassed and has never ceased to excite and amaze."[16]

In Constantinople, standard building materials consisted of stone, brick, and lime mortars, combined with marble and other decorative elements, the latter usually taken from older buildings. Roofs were covered with ceramic or stone tile, or with lead sheeting. Brick-making was a major industry during all the Byzantine centuries. Brick-makers mixed clay with water in a pit, allowing it to sit for anywhere between twelve hours and a week. Then they added sand, put the wet clay in mold; and laid the bricks on a bed of sand to dry. They fired the bricks in a kiln, or, sometimes, simply built a fire around stacked bricks. In either case, the fire had to burn for at least twelve hours and be constantly tended in order to reach the correct temperature. Mortar was manufactured by heating limestone to 1,000 degrees and hydrating the resulting quicklime with water to create a binding agent that was mixed with aggregates, such as sand, pebbles, or crushed brick.[17]

Focusing on small-scale architecture from the ninth to the fifteenth centuries, Robert Ousterhout elucidated the methods of Byzantine masons. Trained in workshops, they based their work on hands-on practice rather than abstract theory. Unlike ancient architects and those of late antiquity, they do not appear to have used drawings. Rather, they would begin by marking the plan on the ground with stones, and then laying it out full-scale with ropes. Design and construction went hand-in-hand. Masons typically made walls by alternating bands of brick and stone, but constructed vaults and domes of brick and mortar alone. Often, they would build the scaffolding into walls as they constructed them. When the building was completed, they either would remove the scaffolding and fill the anchoring holes, or else leave it in place for painters and mosaicists to complete their own work. The mason who built a structure and the decorator who added paintings and mosaics were sometimes one and the same.[18]

Interior decorations were integral to Byzantine churches. Sometimes these took the form of revetments—marble panels of various colors and patterns cut in regular shapes and attached to the wall in decorative patterns. The vaulting and upper walls were usually decorated with mosaics made with tesserae, small cubes of colored stone, marble, glass, or terracotta. (See Figures 1, 45, 46, and 48.) Most mosaics had a gold background that was fabricated with clear glass tesserae backed with gold leaf, each piece forming a tiny mirror reflecting light. Tesserae were often set at angles to take advantage of natural light. For fresco paintings, walls were prepared in a similar manner.[19]

15

COMMERCE, CRAFTS, AND MANUFACTURE

Centralized administration was instrumental in the regulation of commerce and manufacture throughout the empire. Villages were closely connected to market towns, which in turn were linked to Constantinople. The Byzantines improved the Roman road system and maintained a merchant fleet, thereby facilitating communication between far-flung regions. Emperors continually sought to consolidate state control in order to increase the flow of tax monies, essential for maintaining the large bureaucracy and the army. They tried to keep the peace in Constantinople by making cheap foodstuffs and essential goods readily available. Unlike any other early medieval society, Byzantine manufacture and commerce were facilitated by means of an uninterrupted exchange of currency.[20]

Merchants and artisans were not always sharply distinguished. Artisans often sold their own goods in local markets, where they rented space under the colonnades. Such goods included jewelry, glassware, and pottery; textiles, perfumes, and leatherwork; and baked bread, olive oil, vegetable oil, and other foodstuffs. Artisan trades also included carpentry, masonry, and building construction, along with ivory carving, painting, book illustration, and making mosaics. Though evidence about gender roles is often lacking, craft apprenticeship and production were no doubt influenced by gender. Women made cloth not only for their own families, but on a larger scale in urban workshops. They worked with their husbands in family workshops, and they were active as vendors in local markets. As the Byzantine cities recovered their vitality in the ninth and tenth centuries, urban markets were augmented by market fairs in the provinces. Provincials also came to Constantinople in order to sell products such as linen. Always, artisans were monitored by the city prefect, the Eparch of Constantinople.[21]

In Constantinople, many trades were organized into professional guilds that were supervised by the state. An ordinance regulating these guilds appears in a surviving document called *The Book of the Eparch*, dating from the early tenth century. The regulations protected guild members from competition, both from landowners involved in trade and from artisans and merchants outside the guild. They governed the quality and quantity of production, prices, and salaries. They also controlled the activities of foreign traders, and beginning in the tenth century Eparchs began to grant outsiders trading privileges, including Italians from Amalfi and Venice.[22]

One of the most highly developed Byzantine crafts was ivory carving (Figure 6). Obtaining their raw material from the tusks of African elephants, carvers produced exquisite plaques, boxes, and other small objects. They probably worked not in workshops but in their own homes. Many ivories were used as icons, images of venerated figures. After carefully observing the wear patterns of extant ivories, Anthony Cutler concluded that these objects of devotion often were held in the hand and rubbed or kissed. He also concluded that they reveal information about craft methods. Though tool marks are rare because the carver usually polished them away, it is evident that tusks were usually carved with the grain.

16

While the process is not known from actual survivals, the use of a "pick-like or chisel edged tool" must be assumed. Artisans carved plaques from the large part of the tusk, applying their tools at different angles a number of times and smoothing their work with successively finer files. After sketching human figures with ink or a graver, they struck the outlines, perhaps with a straight-edged chisel, and then carved them. Detailing required the use of a fine blade or pick for delicate lines such as facial features and folding drapery. Finishing involved polishing the plaques, both to remove tool marks and to enhance the contrast between details and background, and sometimes coloring.[23]

Byzantine craftsmen created for their lay clientele religious plaques of extraordinary workmanship, along with icons (wooden panels painted with images), mosaics, frescos, and painted miniatures in books that often depicted images of Christ, Mary, and the saints. Between about 725 and 843, however, many such images were destroyed during the period of "iconoclasm." The reasons for Byzantine iconoclasm must be related to the military and political instability of the empire during this period as well as to the belief that such depictions amounted to the veneration of images, prohibited by Biblical precept; it is relevant that Jewish and Islamic theology both involved similar proscriptions. A succession of Byzantine emperors waged campaigns against the veneration of images, ordering icons to be destroyed. Even though the iconoclasts were not opposed to images per se—often replacing religious icons with representations of animals, plants and secular themes such as hunting—thousands of icons were "broken, burned, painted over, and exposed to many insults," while image-worshipers were banished, imprisoned, and even executed. Then, iconoclasm ended as it had begun—by the order of an emperor who declared it to be heretical.[24]

Figure 6. *Late-tenth-century Byzantine ivory. Central triptych panel with The Crucifixion. Courtesy The Walters Art Museum, Baltimore, Maryland.*

From the point of view of the Byzantine state, one of the most important craft traditions was silk manufacture. Silk was a precious commodity and also a symbol of authority. The highest grades of silk clothed the imperial family and its court, as well as church officials. The precise origins of Byzantine sericulture—the name given to the raising of silkworms—are matters of speculation and debate. Stories about it beginning after silkworm cocoons were smuggled into Byzantine territory have been rejected as too simplistic, especially considering that the production of high-quality silk thread is a complicated process that simply could not have sprung from the mere availability of cocoons. However it began, by the seventh century silk production was a principal feature of the Byzantine economy. Women carried out a significant part of the labor, attending to moriculture, the cultivation of mulberry trees, in diverse areas of the empire—Syria, Asia Minor, southern Greece, Italy, Phoenicia, Egypt. But the heart of the industry was Constantinople, where silk cloth was made both in imperial factories and in private workshops.[25]

Moriculture, sericulture, the processing of cocoons, and, finally, the production of high-quality yarn were complex procedures requiring great skill. Sericulture, for example, necessitated cutting mulberry leaves to the correct size from the time cocoons hatched until their full development; feeding in a rearing house every two hours, day and night; and enlarging the trays as the worms grew to prevent overcrowding. Cocoon production required setting up spinning boards, mounting silkworms ready to spin, and allowing some moths to emerge and mate. For the spinning of yarn, control of noise, humidity, and temperature were all crucial factors. Spinning boards had to be dismantled at the proper time. Cocoons had to be gathered and graded, and they could be stored only for short periods.[26]

Yarn production involved vat tenders who boiled the cocoons and reelers who unwound the silk threads. Waste silk or floss had to be spun rather than reeled. Reeling could produce some twist, making the thread stronger, but threads to be used for the foundation layer of the loom—the warp threads—had to be twisted further by hand or on a spindle wheel. At this point the yarn could be dyed. Then it was ready for imperial or private silk weavers, or for wealthy individuals who had weaving done for them in their own homes. Besides the weavers, a weaving workshop required carpenters to make the looms, pattern-makers to create the motifs for weaving, drawboys to operate the device that produced figures on the woven cloth, embroiderers, printers and finally, tailors of silk clothing. There were probably different types of draw looms for different patterns and sorts of weaving, but their precise structure and development remains a topic of ongoing study and discussion among scholars.[27]

A particular kind of artifact—a lead seal—has provided fascinating insight into commerce in Byzantine silk. As Nicolas Oikonomidès explained, most Byzantine officials possessed a type of iron pincers called a *boulloterion* with which to make seals. The ends, which were inscribed with writing or signs, were pressed on roundels of lead to make seals for letters and official documents. For the most part, only seals directly authorized by the head of state had an effigy of the emperor or empress. Pieces of burlap on extant seals make it evident that officials called a *commerciarii* used seals with such an effigy on bales of merchandise. Because numerous seals can be dated, Oikonomidès argued that the *commerciarii* were dealing in silk bales, and that their seals guaranteed that the sale was authorized and that the quality of the silk was acceptable. On the basis of this evidence, he traced the vicissitudes of the silk trade and the degree of state control. By the ninth and tenth centuries, what had been "a state monopoly accessible to a few privileged individuals" was becoming "the privilege of a whole group of professionals whose activities, motivated by profit, were regulated and protected by the state." This trend, he concludes, points to the flourishing urban economies that would develop in eleventh-century Byzantium. Other historians have argued that the *commerciarii* functioned much more broadly than as dealers of silk only, including an important role in supplying the army.[28]

* * *

Although certain aspects of the relationship between technology, society, and Byzantine culture were unique to Byzantium, needless to say the empire did not exist in isolation. Its history must be considered in the context of complex relationships, both hostile and friendly, with the Arabs and with the European west. Three aspects of Byzantine society, each with a fundamental technological component, will be treated in later chapters of this booklet in the context of those relationships: military technologies, transportation technologies, and communication. But, now, we turn from the Byzantine Empire to the Arab territories whose culture came to be focused on the new religion of Islam.

19

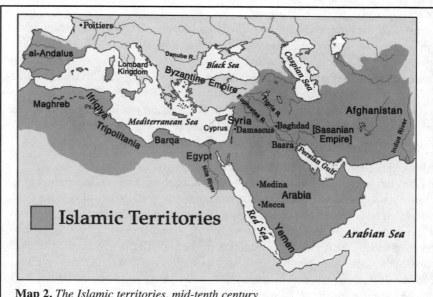

Map 2. *The Islamic territories, mid-tenth century.*

TECHNOLOGY IN THE ISLAMIC STATES

The rise of Islam and the Arab conquests of the seventh and early eighth centuries were remarkable historical events. In the hundred years after the death of the prophet Muhammad in 632, Islamic power was extended from India to Spain, while the extent of Byzantine power was severely curtailed. The Arab advance was stopped only in southern France by the Battle of Poitiers in 732. Historians have long debated the significance of the early Islamic conquests, but, as Fred McGraw Donner points out, expansion entailed two separate phenomena—first the conquests, namely the extension of Islamic power over new territories, and second, Arab migration, the movement of Arabic-speaking peoples from the Arabian peninsula into the new territories.[1]

More than anything else, the availability of water shaped the life and technologies of the Arab peoples. Yemen, in Southwest Arabia, received enough rainfall to support farming with the aid of extensive irrigation—that is, the artificial distribution of water by means of dams, cisterns, channels, and ditches. This agriculture allowed a fairly dense population and enabled the development of towns, crafts, and commerce. Elsewhere on the peninsula the rainfall was too sparse for irrigation agriculture, but the desert was interspersed with places that contained springs or aquifers that could be tapped by wells. These oases, as they were called, supported small settlements of people who cultivated date palms. There were also a few large oases that supported larger populations including artisans and merchants, with water sufficient for the cultivation of thousands of date palms.[2]

Outside of the oases, camel nomads lived in "tenting groups" numbering five to twenty people and joined with other groups of near-kinsmen at various times during the year. They survived, often at subsistence levels, on milk from their camels and foodstuffs that they could obtain in trade with oasis settlements. They also acquired weapons and took great pride in their martial skills, attacking rival nomadic groups and raiding settlements, taking goods or exacting tribute. In *The Camel and the Wheel*, Richard Bulliet analyzed the historical context in which camel nomads acquired political, military, and economic power. He argued that their ascendancy had a crucial technological element—the invention of the north Arabian camel saddle, which enabled them to become effective fighters and thereby shift the balance of political power in their own favor. Eventually, this led to their social and economic integration with settled communities. The rising power of camel nomads had a striking ramification in the medieval centuries, namely the abandonment of wheeled vehicles in Arabia and eventually throughout an immense area from the eastern Mediterranean across northern Africa. Instead of wheeled vehicles, the camel became the essential mode of transport.[3]

While nomads controlled the deserts, religious aristocracies controlled towns and settlements, empowered by the respect of tribal groups for the sanctuaries they maintained for the honor and worship of the gods. Those who entered sacred places were bound by rules of conduct which included the prohibition of killing. Towns with major sanctuaries often became important trading centers because of their relative safety. In the sixth century, Mecca was such a religious sanctuary, its shrine, the Ka'aba, attracting pilgrims from all over the peninsula. The fairs at Mecca also made it a significant destination for caravans. Meccans carried goods that had come from Africa or the Far East—including cloth, leather, and slaves—to Syria. Back from Syria to Mecca they carried wine, grains, and weapons. Mecca became a cosmopolitan city where tribal loyalties were weakened as many sorts of people congregated, including exiles and foreigners. Muhammad was born into one of the clans of Mecca, a family of traders. As a young man he worked as a caravaner.[4]

The rise of Islam and the Islamic conquests transformed Arab tribal society even as it profoundly influenced conquered lands. Islam allowed the inclusion of individuals who had been marginalized by tribal hierarchies, and substituted a universalizing, monotheistic religion for tribal loyalties. Religion and politics went hand in hand; for the first time, the Arabian peninsula as a whole became a state. Although the new religion had only a tenuous hold at the time of Muhammad's death in 632, it was soon consolidated by men who called themselves his successors or *caliphs*. Subsequent Islamic conquests did not involve proselytizing efforts by the Arabs. Rather, Arabic military elites conquered opposing armies and then established control over indigenous peoples. While these peoples were often forced to pay tribute, their administrative, economic, and political institutions frequently remained intact, and many of them converted to Islam only gradually over several centuries. The Arabs assimilated into the cultures into which they had moved, as they also changed those cultures. Islamic hegemony was accompanied by the Arab adoption of numerous crafts and technologies originally unknown to them.[5]

AGRICULTURE AND IRRIGATION

As the Arabs conquered new lands, they adopted and sometimes changed existing patterns of land tenure. An example is the Sasanian Empire where, in the fifth and sixth centuries, land transfers increasingly involved large village estates bought and sold by members of a landed aristocracy. By the late Sasanian period most of the peasant-cultivators were losing title to the land that they worked, and the Islamic conquest did not immediately change this situation. By the second half of the seventh century, numerous Arabic aristocrats held village estates as absentee landlords.[6]

Agricultural labor was performed by tenants. Most tenancy took the form of sharecropping or renting. Renters leased the land for a fixed annual amount, measured either in cash or in produce. Sharecropping was an arrangement whereby peasants held a permanent lease on the land and could decide what crops to grow, could sublet the land to others, and could pass on these rights to successors. In return, they were obliged to give between a quarter and a third of the crop to their landlord. In addition to tenancy, there is evidence for the widespread use of slaves on large estates. Most were Greeks, probably from Syria, captured by the Sasanians in their wars with the Byzantines and then acquired (along with the land itself) by the new Islamic rulers.[7]

The Sasanians had maintained irrigation systems throughout much of the land. On the large rivers they had built substantial dams. On the plateau they had constructed *qanats* (Figure 7). A *qanat* is an underground canal which slopes downward from the surface until it reaches under the aquifer—the underground layer of soil, stone, and gravel commonly known as the water table. Water would seep from the aquifer into the canal and then flow out into an above-ground irrigation channel. To ventilate the tunnel and to enable the excavation of soil, vertical airshafts were sunk every 20 to 150 yards.[8]

The Arab conquerors used the existing Sasanian infrastructure, including *qanats* and other irrigation structures, as they built new garrisons. Some of these sites developed into cities, such as Basra and Baghdad, which attracted traders and visitors from throughout the Islamic lands. An expanding urbanism resulted in the growth of cities serving the Arab elite that required reliable supplies of food and water. To this end, the Arabs granted large expanses of swampland to individuals—usually clients of Arab governors—who drained and developed them for cultivation. They built extensive canal systems that changed swamps

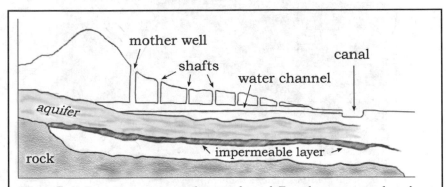

Figure 7. *A Sasanian* qanat, *or underground canal. To make a* qanat, *workers dug a trial shaft to make sure of the presence and depth of the groundwater table. When they reached water, they determined whether it had a constant flow and was located in an impermeable stratum. If so, they ascertained the correct slope to ensure the proper rate of flow from that point to the surface. Actual work usually began at the surface end and proceeded backwards. Great care had to be taken when the water-bearing section was entered to prevent breakage by a rush of water.*

into farms, thereby providing foodstuffs for the new cities. Sometimes Arab rulers themselves built new canals to provide water for urban populations and to irrigate fields.[9]

In most of their new lands, the Arabs encouraged the continued use of technologies already established. For example, Egyptian agricultural technologies were dominated by the annual flooding of the Nile. The height reached by the annual flooding was a matter of intense concern. If the river failed to rise to "sixteen arms," the amount of land inundated would be insufficient and famine would result. Floodwaters were controlled to some extent by dams and canals that dated to pre-Islamic and early Islamic centuries. Sultans built and maintained the main canals, while village headmen took charge of small dams and canals that diverted water from one field to the next. The peasants (called *fellaheen*) participated in the ongoing labor of dredging the canals with teams of oxen and removing weeds and debris with pickaxes and hoes. Winter crops such as wheat, barley, lentils, beans, bitter vetch (a plant used for fodder), and flax were irrigated by the Nile floodwaters alone. Summer crops, including cotton, melons, sesame, and sugarcane, were cultivated with the aid of water-lifting devices such as the *shaduf* (see Figure 8) and the waterwheel, the general term for which is the *noria*.[10]

Figure 8. *Drawing water from the Nile for irrigation with a* shaduf. *The* shaduf *consists of a long beam that rests on a horizontal crossbar in a lever arrangement. On one end of the beam hangs another long beam or a rope to which is attached a bucket. At the other end is a counterweight. The worker pulls down the vertical pole or rope until the bucket goes into the water and fills it. Then the worker pushes it up, and with the help of the counterweight, turns it, and dumps the water into the irrigation canal. Photo credit: ErichLessing/Art Resource.*

One type of wheel, often called a *saqiya*, was turned by an animal. Goaded by a peasant, the animal—ox, donkey, or camel hitched to a shaft—turned a horizontal "lantern" pinion which engaged the cogs of a vertical wheel, the lower part of which was immersed in a source of water. Pots were attached to the rim of the vertical wheel, called a potgarland wheel. (See Figures 9 and 10.) As the pots turned on the wheel, they reached the water upside down, scooped up the water and then, as they reached the top again, dumped it into a canal or trough.[11]

With variations, these water-lifting technologies came to be used throughout all Islamic lands, including the Iberian Peninsula. The peninsula was called al-Andalus after it was conquered by Arabs leading a Berber horse cavalry in 711. (The Berbers were a people who lived in the area of present-day Morocco.) Thomas Glick describes the region as being influenced by two cultural and ecological systems, one dominated by the Christians in the north and the other by the Muslims. Arab influence on agriculture and technology was particularly notable. Because the entire Mediterranean basin is similar, the Arabs were familiar with the environment of their new lands and could readily import agricultural technologies to al-Andalus that they had used elsewhere. Glick points to the "extensive Syrianization of the landscape that took place in the eighth century," including the migration of Syrian people and the importation of Syrian agricultural systems, hydraulic machinery, and plants.[12]

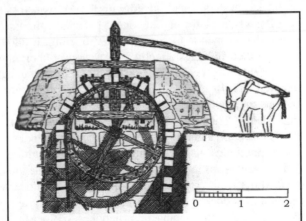

Figure 9. *A* saqiya *as depicted in 1955 at Ibiza in the Balearic Islands, Spain. The wheel with pots is called a potgarland wheel. As it turned, pots on the bottom entered the water mouth first, scooped it up, arrived at the top of the wheel, and then dumped the water into an irrigation channel or trough. A device called a pawl acted on the cogs of the potgarland wheel to prevent it from going into reverse when the animal was unhitched. From Thorkild Schiøler,* **Roman and Islamic Water-Lifting Wheels** *(Odense: Odense Universitets Forlag, 1973), 17. Courtesy Thorkild Schiøler.*

25

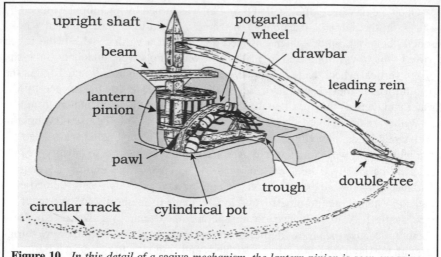

Figure 10. *In this detail of a* saqiya *mechanism, the lantern pinion is seen engaging the cogs of the vertical wheel. From Thorkild Schiøler,* **Roman and Islamic Water-Lifting Wheels** *(Odense: Odense Universitets, 1973), 16. Courtesy Thorkild Schiøler.*

In the figure, the labels read: upright shaft, potgarland wheel, beam, drawbar, leading rein, lantern pinion, pawl, trough, double-tree, circular track, cylindrical pot.

Particularly important in al-Andalus was the animal-powered *noria*, which probably originated in Persia and moved with the Arabs across northern Africa to the Iberian Peninsula by the eighth century. Because the *noria* was a highly efficient device that cost little to construct and operate, it allowed small land-holders to exploit their holdings effectively. A second important hydraulic technology in al-Andalus was the *qanat,* which had several advantages over surface canals; it required less slope, did not lose water by evaporation, and obviated the necessity of constructing lifting devices.[13]

After the Islamic conquests, migration and travel were relatively easy throughout a vast region, and this had important consequences for the transmission of new technologies and new knowledge. In agriculture, it enabled the establishment of new crops throughout Islamic lands, a phenomenon that historians have called the Arab "green revolution." These included rice, sorghum (a cereal grass used as fodder and for making molasses or syrup), sugarcane, cotton, watermelons, eggplants, spinach, artichokes, colocasia (the tubers and leaves of which are cooked and eaten), sour oranges, lemons, limes, bananas, plantains, mangoes, and coconut palms. Many of these crops were originally from India or from further east. Most were summertime crops. Their successful cultivation required numerous plantings, meticulous irrigation, and plowing techniques that conserved the water in the soil.[14]

The westward movement of many of these plants began in pre-Islamic times but did not get far. Increased travel and migration across Islamic lands encouraged plant diffusion, however, since people going from east to west would naturally have brought their eating habits with them, and peasants may well have carried the seeds and cuttings, along with the knowledge necessary for establishing new crops. Establishing a new crop involved innovations in both cultivation and patterns of consumption. Often it required the extension and improvement of irrigation, and improved irrigation techniques were widespread in the medieval Islamic world. New summer plantings greatly increased the productivity of the land. Sometimes a number of plantings on the same plot of land could be made in one summer. Careful attention to the suitability of particular soils to particular plants, fertilization with human and animal waste and other materials, and even the development of new varieties of plants that were more suitable to the new conditions—all played a part in this "green revolution." The result was an increased food supply leading to population growth and growing urbanization.[15]

ARCHITECTURE AND BUILDING CONSTRUCTION

Ernst J. Grube described some general characteristics of Islamic architecture, whether religious or secular, public or private—mosques, tombs, dwellings. First is the emphasis on enclosed spaces. The traditional Muslim house presents the street with high windowless walls, and some structures are completely hidden by other buildings. If a building displays a visible facade, it often reveals little about the interior. Accompanying the idea of a "hidden architecture" is the absence of any correlation between architectural forms and function. An example is the four-*iwan* courtyard structure that was common in the Sasanian Empire and subsequently adopted by Islamic architects (Figure 11). The *iwan* is a vaulted hall that is walled on three sides. In a four-*iwan* structure, four such halls surround a square, making a central courtyard. This structure was (and is) used throughout the Islamic world in mosques, palaces, *madrasas* (schools attached to mosques), and caravansaries (overnight shelters for caravans).[16]

A second major type of architectural plan is the hypostyle or arcaded plan, of which the Great Mosque of Cordoba is an example (Figure 12). In this plan there is a courtyard in the center and "a forest of columns" that form arcades or colonnades, all covered by a wood-beam roof. It has the advantage of simplicity, and only necessitates repetitions of a post-and-lintel structures (horizontal beams on vertical supports). Domes projecting up from flat roofs were later added to many such buildings.[17]

With the exception of the *iwan* court plan, as Grube explains, Islamic architecture rarely consisted of a focused unit in which the form of the building reflected the functions of its parts. For example, the center of a mosque—the prayer niche or *mihrab*—while always oriented in the direction of Mecca, did not have any particular set position that was indicated by the interior space of the building. This is sharply different from western European practice, where the altar of a church was always built in a predetermined space. In contrast, Islamic buildings were often designed with a deliberate disconnect between form and function. Because many of the buildings did not have a set orientation, it was easy to construct additions facing in any direction without destroying any preexisting balance. Interior decoration was highly significant. In Grube's words, the decoration of interior spaces was "a true negation of architecture as conceived in Europe, that is, of structure; it

27

Figure 11. *The courtyard of the Great Mosque of Kairouan (Qayrawan) in Tunisia, founded by Prince Ziyada Allah in 836. The minaret dates from that year, the courtyard and arcades from 862–75. This is an example of the* Iwan *structure. Photo credit: Erich Lessing/Art Resource, New York.*

aims at a visual negation of the reality of weight and the necessity of support." For example, heavy, weight-bearing piers might be made to look ephemeral with lace-like ornamentation. Such effects were achieved with surface decorations made of tiles, mosaics, painted designs, molded plaster, and open cut work in walls and vaults. (See Figure 13.) All of these motifs were applied with a rich repertory of geometric and floral designs, inscriptions, and calligraphy.[18]

Most surviving Muslim buildings from the medieval centuries are mosques. Building styles and materials depended upon the location and the availability of materials. In Syria, for example, traditional ashlar masonry persisted in Islamic times because of the availability of Syrian limestone that was extremely durable but at the same time easy to work. Building walls of pounded clay (to be discussed below) occurred in areas where fieldstone was lacking. The building trades were highly specialized. Stoneworkers were divided into quarrymen and masons. Masons were separated into those who prepared rough blocks for inner walls and

Figure 12. *The Great Mosque, Cordoba, Spain, built in the hypostyle or arcaded architectural style. Photo credit: Art Resource, New York.*

foundations, those who produced finished ashlar, and skilled carvers. Woodworkers included sawyers who cut rough timber to the correct dimensions, carpenters who did woodwork inside buildings, turners who made wooden screens for windows and other ornamental woodwork, and craftsmen who fabricated chests and door locks. Specialization facilitated the rapid completion of building projects. Standards of workmanship were guaranteed by craft and market laws administered by an urban and market magistrate called a *muhtasib*, whose modus operandi—as we know from surviving market manuals—was similar to that of the Byzantine *eparch*.[19]

Masons often used granite or basalt for the foundations of buildings. Workers prepared mortar from either gypsum (plaster of Paris) or lime. Often they constructed buildings with the ground floor and perhaps a second floor of stone and the higher stories of brick. They might use columns and capitals from old buildings, but not in their original function; for example, they would invert a capital and use it as the base for a shaft. Often they reinforced columns and shafts with iron rods. They made buildings with intricately patterned and colored stonework, and marble carved into complex shapes.[20]

A second major building material was brick. Brick-making had

Figure 13. *Decorated surfaces in the Alhambra, Grenada, Spain, built between 1338 and 1390. Photo credit: Steven A. Walton.*

reached a high level of refinement by the Sasanids in Iran, and many Sasanid techniques were adopted in the Islamic era. Builders used baked bricks for permanent buildings, but also used unbaked bricks at the building site, mixing clay with water and straw and tramping on it with bare feet before putting it in wooden molds; they turned the bricks at set intervals until they dried. Making baked bricks entailed more care in mixing clay and sand with water. These were also dried in the sun, but afterwards they were packed into a kiln and fired for three days. Fuel included shrubs and dried camel dung. Brick-makers used gypsum mortar for baked bricks except in exposed areas, where they used a lime-sand mortar. For ornamental work, bricks were cut into molds shaped as polygons or stars, the surfaces polished with a hard stone, and then they were put into a wood frame in a decorative design and covered with gypsum plaster. When this dried, workers lifted the panel from the frame and placed it into position in the building.[21]

A third building technique consisted of clay walling or *tapia*, constructed without the use of bricks. In one method two wooden walls were set on a foundation with space between them, and rope or twine holding them in position. Workers then

Figure 14. *A barrel vault and groined vault.*

put earth mixed with quick-lime into this form and pounded it. When one course was finished they moved the form up for the next. In another method, walls were constructed layer by layer without forms. As they reached higher, walls got thinner and leaned slightly inward. Then, when cracking occurred, a building in effect consolidated itself. Doorways and windows were reinforced with stone slabs or timber. Walls were waterproofed by capping them with lime, sometimes over a layer of poles.[22]

Initially, Islamic architects constructed rounded arches adopted from Roman and Byzantine precedents. But their desire for novelty led them to develop the pointed arch and other arches in a great variety of shapes. They often reinforced arches with timber tie-rods. Because of the scarcity of timber, they also developed a variety of vaults and domes that required little or no wooden centering to support the structure as they were building it. These included barrel vaults and an inter-secting variant called groined vaults. (See Figure 14.) They also developed diverse methods for making the transition from rectangular or square walls to a dome. Byzantine and Sasanid solutions to this challenge included the pendentive used in Hagia Sophia, but Muslim architects also developed domes with ribbed vaulting and double-shell construction, making domes lighter and thereby allowing a larger structure.[23]

A scholar who has investigated the development of the medieval Islamic town and city, Hugh Kennedy, outlined the profound changes that occurred in Syrian cities under Islamic rule. The wide streets and colonnades, theaters and baths, and market squares (the *agora*) that characterized the ancient city slowly disap-peared in a process that had begun even before the rise of Islam. In the Islamic city, commercial establishments were located in linear fashion along narrow streets. As a public meeting place, the mosque superseded the *agora* and theater. Roman law had emphasized the distinction between the state and private prop-erty, the state protecting public domains from private incursions. In Islamic law, by contrast, the family and the house were of central importance. Owners of houses could build out, just so long as the construction did not disturb the neigh-bors. Streets were only wide enough for two pack animals to pass. Richard Bulliet has suggested that the form of the Islamic city, with its narrow winding streets, is one result of the disappearance of wheeled transport between the fourth and eighth centuries.[24]

30

The textile industry was basic to the economy of the Islamic world, as it was in the Byzantine Empire and in western Europe. Especially in Islamic regions, textiles were used not only for clothing but also for tents, rugs, and wall hangings. The scarcity of wood in the eastern Mediterranean was conducive to the use of rugs and wall hangings in place of wooden furniture. Rugs were portable and could be moved around in order to change part of a dwelling from a sitting area to a dining area to sleeping quarters. Nomads used textiles for bags in which to carry goods and also for their tents. Clothing was made according to the customs of particular locations and norms of gender, class, and status. The four primary fibers used for textiles were wool and linen, native to the Mediterranean, and silk and cotton, both originating in Asia. Secondary fibers such as hemp also were used, as well as a variety of mixed fibers such as linen and silk blends.[25]

In pre-Islamic times, linen was made in Egypt and valued by the Arabs as well as by the Byzantine rulers of Egypt. For centuries, it was the staple cloth of Islamic lands. Linen is made from flax, which was grown in upper Egypt. When the Arabs conquered Egyptian lands they inherited a flourishing linen industry located in the towns and villages of lower Egypt. Egyptian weavers produced both ordinary linens in white and colors, and fine linens, including rich brocades. The Persian town of Fars also produced fine linens, and particularly in the tenth and eleventh centuries linen factories in this area of the old Sasanian Empire produced and exported cloth of very high quality.[26]

To derive usable fibers from flax, workers dried the stalks, fermented them in water, dried them again, and then placed them on stone or wooden blocks and pounded them with mallets. They then combed the stalks to remove any remaining woody material and separate the bundles of fibers. They spun the fibers into long threads and wove them into cloth, usually on stationary vertical looms that were used by settled Islamic populations. Linen is a versatile cloth, fine enough for veils and strong enough for ropes. Its gray-brown fibers must be bleached and it is difficult to dye, however. So, when decorative colors were desired, workers often mixed the linen with another kind of fiber, such as cotton or silk.[27]

Cotton is native to India but had spread westward to some extent before the Islamic conquests. During Islamic rule, Iraq, Syria, and Yemen in southwest Arabia became major centers of cotton production. Cotton was used for making cloth, but also for stuffing quilts, mattresses, and pillows. Like linen, cotton is a plant product. Textile workers began cotton processing by beating the "bolls" to remove the seeds, after which they proceeded to the processes of carding, spinning, weaving, dyeing, and finishing. Cotton was versatile and could be used for a variety of cloth from fine gauze to thick fabrics similar to wool. The availability of both linen and cotton cloth (and therefore rags) provided the raw materials for the production of paper, an important product of medieval Islamic lands, as will be discussed in chapter six.[28]

Silk was used as a luxury fabric. As we have seen, silk was a highly developed Byzantine industry. When the Arabs conquered Syria, they took over the industry there and expanded it. Sericulture gradually spread throughout Islamic lands and into western Europe. Weaving intricate patterns in silk was made possible by the development of the drawloom, with which workers used fine strings instead of wooden heddles to raise and lower the warp threads to create the shed. Several thousand drawstrings could be used, each one controlling a single warp thread. A drawloom required two workers, a weaver and a drawboy who sat on a platform on top of the loom, watched the pattern the weaver was creating, and drew up the correct strings in succession, making the sheds through which the weaver passed the shuttle. Around the year 1000, a new technique was developed called *lampas*, which speeded the process of making highly decorated weaves by using two sets of warps and wefts and enabling the creation of patterns and ground weaves that were separate.[29]

The relationship of political power and textiles was highly significant in the medieval Islamic world. This is especially evident in the *tiraz* system initiated in the late seventh century. (*Tiraz* is an Arabic word derived from a Persian word for embroidery.) In this system state workshops first produced long, beautifully worked strips embroidered with the ruler's name and other information, and later all manner of cloth and clothing. The ruler distributed coats, shirts, tunics, caftans, pants, turbans, and other items of clothing to individuals who were members of his court. Thus did an individual's apparel signify his or her close connection to the highest power.[30]

In addition to textiles, artisans produced artifacts out of pottery, glass, and metal, crafts that entailed transforming materials from the earth—clay, sand, and ores. Specialists fabricated many kinds of containers from these materials, as well as armor, weapons, tools, utensils, precision instruments, coins, and jewelry.[31]

Potters collected clay from riverbanks. By the twelfth century, they were also making a potting material by grinding together sand, quartz, and other substances, and then mixing them with water to make a stone-paste or frit ware. Potting techniques included modeling slabs and coils of clay by hand, pressing clay into preformed molds, and throwing—shaping the clay on a potter's wheel. Shaped objects were left to dry in the sun and then fired in a kiln. Particularly important in the dry climates of the eastern Mediterranean were earthenware vessels for the storage of water. One special type, called *gadus*, was the pot used for the potgarland wheel of the *saqiya*. Pots for water were porous, causing evaporation on the surface, thereby cooling the vessel and its contents. But such pots were unsuitable for olive oil, which turns rancid with long exposure to air. A glaze applied to an earthenware vessel or tile functions as a seal, and potters made glazes by adding red lead, which lowers the temperature at which the glaze mixture turns into glass. In the twelfth century, an alkaline glaze similar to glass was developed; it was made from a mixture of soda or potash, to which salt sometimes was added. Glazes could be colored and decorated, a technique leading to the development of fine ceramic wares. Abbasid rulers of the eighth and ninth centuries particularly admired such wares from China, and Islamic potters refined their own craft partly in response to these wares from the east, developing stone-paste as part of their art.[32]

Metal was worked by specialists who made utensils and vessels, arms and armor, jewelry, tools, and scientific instruments, each of which involved different traditions, workshops, and techniques. They created objects from silver, gold, and copper alloys, primarily an alloy of copper and zinc called brass. Bronze, an alloy of copper and tin, was rare and expensive in the Islamic world because of the high cost of tin, which had to be imported from England or Asia. Metalworkers used two general techniques. In casting, they poured molten metal into a form. They also worked metal by hammering, forging, or spinning on a lathe, a device developed in the early thirteenth century. Brass objects such as incense burners and ewers for water were often highly decorated, and metalworkers were ultimately able to transform brass objects into luxury goods by pressing wires into them and creating inlays that made them resemble those made of gold and silver.[33]

WORK AND GENDER

Around 1890, a vast collection of documents relating to the medieval Islamic world was found in Fustat (now called Old Cairo), in a *geniza* connected to a synagogue. *Geniza* is a Hebrew word meaning a storehouse or treasure. The Jews believed that writings in which the name of God appeared (or even documents written in Hebrew) should be buried in a cemetery. As a result, a Jewish community in medieval Fustat placed thousands of documents intended for later burial in a lumber-room connected to their synagogue. Long afterward, a renovation of the synagogue revealed the sealed room containing—as it was gradually realized—a priceless collection of documents concerning work, marriage, and commerce; letters; wills; and literary materials. These documents provide detailed accounts of daily life, work, and commerce as it pertained to this Egyptian Jewish community, especially from the eleventh to the thirteenth centuries.[34]

From the Geniza documents, scholars have learned that the typical workplace was a shop headed by "a single craftsman, a family, a clan, or a number of partners, usually not more than five." Two new industries—sugar-making and papermaking—that used techniques of Chinese origin involved a greater concentration of manpower than was the case in older craft industries. In Islamic lands, both industries used vertical waterwheels and cams to macerate the fibers and cane respectively. While the crafts in Islamic lands had not yet been organized into guilds (this occurred only in the fourteenth century), the practitioners of particular crafts concentrated together in the same locality. Thus streets or quarters were named after "clothiers, tailors, perfumers, coppersmiths, turners, chest makers, woolworkers, manufacturers of leather bottles, makers of almond sweetmeats, oil makers." Often the same worker who made a product also sold it.[35]

Although craft-workers were from the lower strata of society, skilled artisans were respected and manual work was not considered degrading. The Geniza documents reveal a high degree of specialization. The most important industries concerned textiles, dyeing, and clothing; metals, glass, and pottery; and building construction and food processing. There were specialists in numerous small trades: makers of kohl sticks used to apply eyelid powder; makers of writing cases, mirrors, mats, fans, spindles, sieves, combs for hair and flax; makers of beads; perforators of pearls; persons who processed corals. In every household, at least one woman worked as a spinner.[36]

33

In a comprehensive study in which she analyzed sources including S. D. Goitein's work on the Geniza documents, Maya Schatzmiller investigated occupations in the medieval Islamic world. She listed hundreds of occupations that include "extractive" work such as agriculture, mining, and fishing, and trades ranging from dye makers, soap makers, brick makers, and textile workers to food processors such as bakers and sausage makers. This study provides a much-needed foundation for understanding the high degree of work specialization that developed over the medieval centuries. It also provides at least a small window into the elusive but important subject of the trade groups to which various workers belonged and attitudes toward manual and skilled labor in general.[37]

A particularly difficult problem in the study of work in the medieval Islamic world concerns the nature of women's work. For rural women, there is a critical lack of evidence. Shatzmiller suggested that "taking families as a production unit in agricultural pursuits provides too small a group to allow any significant division of labor on the basis of gender to be seen." It is certain that both men and women fully participated in agricultural production. Certainly, however, as in the Byzantine Empire and in the west, there was some division of labor by gender. In other arenas, women's work is well documented. Women took care of silkworms, a labor-intensive task, as we have seen. Women produced and sold radish and linseed oils, and brought chickens, eggs, and wool into towns to sell. Indeed, there is much evidence to show that women were often involved in commercial transactions and also active in investing in rural property. Documents reveal female purchases of irrigation rights, of an orchard, of a date plantation, of a silo, of residential properties, and of slaves.[38]

Documentation for urban female work is more extensive than for rural. In manufacturing, women's basic household skills were expanded to a commercial scale in two fundamental areas, textiles and food. The spinning of flax, wool, cotton, and silk were female monopolies. Women worked as embroiderers, weavers of brocades, and carpet-makers, often with their children working alongside. They also made lace, though commercial weaving was a male occupation. Both men and women worked as dyers. Female trades were transmitted within informal apprenticeship systems in which women trained young girls, including their own daughters.[39]

Women were particularly involved in food processing and food production. Documents attest to female millers, vinegar makers, and makers and sellers of sweets, sweetmeats, and cooked beans. Women were also active in health care, working as physicians, midwives, and wet nurses. Women washed the dead and worked as professional wailers. They worked as launderers and as "combers" and "henna applicators." Educated women acted as court secretaries. There were women calligraphers, poets, and scholars.[40]

Beyond the question of who did what kind of work is the more general question of how labor was perceived in the medieval Islamic world. In pre-Islamic nomadic Arab culture, manual labor—"the work of the blacksmith, the peasant, the goldsmith and the sword maker"—was held in contempt. To some extent, this attitude carried over into Islamic times. In the ninth century, the

34

activity of building construction and the development of skilled crafts brought about a literature in which manual labor was a focus of interest and respect. Nevertheless, labor in general was viewed negatively, while commerce was much more highly regarded. In the ninth and tenth centuries, a form of Sufi mysticism developed in reaction to the luxurious lifestyle of court circles in Basra. It adopted the doctrine of *zuhd*, the renunciation of worldly goods and also the work involved in acquiring them, instead relying on God's favor for basic necessities. This mysticism generated a reaction in the form of a literature that advocated work and extolled its value. A conflict of values concerning work continued to the fourteenth century and beyond.[41]

MECHANICAL DEVICES AND SCIENTIFIC INSTRUMENTS

During the eighth and ninth centuries, Arab scholars undertook a remarkable quest to master the learning of the foreign cultures with which they had come into contact, namely in the Byzantine and Sasanian (Persian) empires and India. Scholars and translators sought out classical Greek and Hellenistic writings as well as texts in Syriac and other languages, making them available to the Islamic world by means of translation into Arabic and extensive commentary. They eventually incorporated the entire corpus of Greek classical learning and wrote original works that extended that learning. Translations included Greek and Hellenistic writings on mechanics and mechanical devices—the pseudo-Aristotelian *Mechanical Problems*, and the writings on mechanical devices by Philo of Alexandria (third century B.C.E.) and Hero of Alexandria (second century C.E.). The *Mechanical Problems*, probably written by a follower of Aristotle in the fourth century B.C.E., defined mechanics as a discipline combining mathematics with physics, or—put in another way—theory (meaning the mathematics of mechanical motion) and practice (actual machines and devices). All such writings had been translated into Arabic by the ninth century.[42]

The Arabic word *hiyal* describes the whole range of topics entailing mechanics and machinery. Based on the Greek sources, an Islamic tradition of writing on such topics emerged during the ninth century. The three Musa brothers—Muhammad, Ahmad, and al-Hasan, known as the Banu Musa—were famous for their engineering works in Baghdad and Samarra, and they also wrote *The Book of Ingenious Devices*. The sons of a noted astronomer, they traveled to the Byzantine Empire to bring back books for translation from Greek or Syriac into Arabic.[43]

The Banu Musa wrote books on mathematics and astronomy as well as on mechanics. *The Book of Ingenious Devices* described six fountains and eighty-three trick vessels: pitchers that do not continue to pour after an interruption, vessels that replenish themselves after a small amount of liquid is removed, vessels from which a mixture of liquids would pour from separate spouts. As Donald Hill explained, such vessels were effected by different combinations of siphons, valves, pulleys, gears, cranks, miniature waterwheels, floats, and balances. Each machine was a kind of automata.[44]

A later book devoted to machines, Ibn al-Razzaz al-Jazari's *The Book of Knowledge of Ingenious Mechanical Devices* was completed in 1206. Al-Jazari was the most important and original author on mechanics in medieval Islamic lands. Most of the devices he described are automata, water clocks, and water-raising machines (Figure 15). These were significant for the development of mechanical technologies; for example, one of them embodies the first known instance of a crank that works as part of a machine (in distinction from hand-operated cranks). Al-Jazari's clocks also embody numerous mechanical concepts and technologies, including "accurate calibration of small orifices; feedback control methods; the use of paper models to establish intricate designs; the use of wooden templates; the static balancing of wheels, the use of laminated timber to minimize warping; one-way hinges; and tipping buckets." None of these machines, however, was conceived solely as a practical device. As George Saliba explained, one objective of those who wrote about machines was to address the Aristotelian problem of how to move from potentiality to actuality by means of mechanical devices.[45] Al-Jazari's interest in both theory and practice was characteristic of the Islamic traditions of mechanics.

Figure 15. *The mechanism of the "water-clock of the peacocks." Al-Jazari instructs that the water-clock is to be built behind a fountain. The action of the clock causes peacocks to come out and squabble every half hour. Al-Jazari,* **Book of Knowledge of Mechanical Processes,** *Saljuq dynasty, 1206. Topkapi Palace Museum, Istanbul, Turkey, thirteenth century. Ms. No. 3472. Photo credit: Giraudon/Art Resource, New York.*

Interest in mechanical devices extended to precision instruments, including the balance and, most importantly, astronomical instruments. Such instruments were described in treatises and they were also fabricated and used in practice. A twelfth-century philosopher, Abul Fath al-Khazini, in his treatise on physics titled *The Book of the Balance of Wisdom* (1121–22) described in detail methods of constructing and using balances to determine weights, including the proportions of weights of specific substances in alloys. His descriptions of instruments include dsmall clepsydras (water clocks) that measured short intervals of time and were used in the study of astronomy.[46]

Islamic technologists and astronomers designed intricate astronomical instruments used in the observatories that were built throughout Islamic lands. One example was a planispheric astrolabe (Figure 16). This instrument consists of "a two-dimensional model of the celestial sphere in relation to the earth, based on the assumption that the earth is the center of the universe." It was constructed by stereographic projection, a geometric method whereby points on the celestial sphere were placed on the flat surface of the instrument. The astrolabe functioned as an observational instrument which enabled astronomers to determine the time of sunrise and sunset and the positions of celestial bodies.[47]

Figure 16. *Hispano-Moorish astrolabe, c. 1260, made of brass and copper. Each part of the astrolabe has a central hole so the parts can be held together with a pin and wedge. Parts include plates engraved to indicate the inhabitable regions of the earth; the rete, the celestial part indicating important stars; and the mater, a brass plate with rim. Inventory no. 43504, Museum of the History of Science, Oxford. Courtesy Museum of the History of Science, Oxford.*

* * *

Islamic conquests and migrations had important consequences for the history of technology. The Arabs permitted established modes of production and their associated technologies to continue in the territories they conquered, adopting and developing them futher. Rather than destroying the Byzantine silk industry in Syria, for example, they expanded it. They learned about new crops in the east and adapted them to new locales in the west. They developed many different kinds of arches and domes; they developed new glazes for pottery. They were receptive to the learned cultures they came upon, translating and assimilating Greek, Syriac, and other ancient writings, and composing original works on the basis of this foundation. Islamic powers, although by no means a single, unified entity, spanned both eastern and western lands. Ultimately, Islamic culture would exert a profound influence on western European Christian culture, to which we now turn.

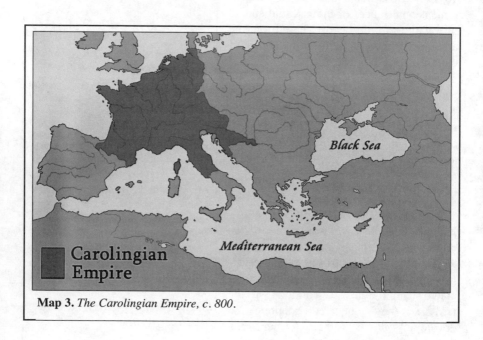

Map 3. *The Carolingian Empire, c. 800.*

TECHNOLOGY IN THE MEDIEVAL WEST

The western Roman Empire disintegrated in the fifth century after a series of migrations and conquests by so-called barbarians, including Goths, Vandals, Huns, Franks, and Lombards. Especially in the Mediterranean regions, Roman legal, political, and social structures often persisted, as did some Roman technologies. Yet many characteristics of the empire were lost, and many others were overlaid by new ones. Although some towns remained, notably in the Lombard region of Italy, for the most part Roman urbanism disappeared.[1]

AGRICULTURE AND THE WORK OF THE COUNTRYSIDE

The early medieval centuries in the west were profoundly rural. Two patterns of settlement and cultivation prevailed. Substantial villages, safer because more easily defensible, developed in regions where the soil was fertile enough to support larger concentrations of people. In regions of poor soil, such as Scotland, Wales, and the highlands of France, dispersed settlements were the rule. Peasants lived on isolated family farms or very small hamlets. They practiced what is called in-field, out-field agriculture. Each household had a small plot of land close to the dwelling (in-field) that was cultivated continuously and fertilized with the waste of humans and farm animals. It also cultivated a plot of land further away (out-field) until it became depleted of nutrients after a year or so. Then they let it lie fallow, using it for grazing (which yielded fertilizer in the form of manure), while they cultivated another plot.[2]

Peasants in the larger villages usually practiced open-field farming. Each village was surrounded by a tract of land that was divided roughly in half. One was planted each year, while the second lay fallow. In northern Europe the field was divided into long narrow strips known as "balks." Each household held a number of strips scattered in each of the two fields. In southern Europe cross-plowing made for rectangular or square fields. In both cases, peasants carried out biennial rotation, planting crops on some lands and letting others lie fallow. In the Mediterranean region peasants used a scratch plow or *sol ard*, discussed in chapter 1 (see figure 4 on page 12). Sometimes it was outfitted with a colter or knife attached to the beam of the plow in order to cut the soil in front of the plowshare, and it made shallow, crisscross furrows, thereby conserving moisture in the dry summers. In the north, the characteristically wet soil made a different sort of plowing advantageous. In the early medieval period, a heavy plow came into use that cut deep furrows and turned the soil, facilitating drainage. The heavy plow had a colter that cut the soil vertically, a plowshare that sliced it horizontally, and a mold-board that flung the slice aside (Figure 17). Heavy plows needed teams of four to eight oxen.[3]

Figure 17. *An image of a man plowing with oxen, begun prior to 1340 for Sir Geoffrey Luttrell. Example of a heavy plow with colter and mold board clearly visible. Luttrell Manuscript, British Library, Ms. Add. 42130, f. 170. Photo credit: Art Resource, New York.*

From the tenth century on, medieval Europe underwent a great increase in agricultural productivity. In his influential *Medieval Technology and Social Change*, Lynn White Jr. argued that this amounted to an "agricultural revolution" engendered by a series of technological innovations. White based his thesis on three related developments: the invention of the heavy, wheeled plow; a traction revolution entailing the invention of the rigid horse collar and the use of horse-shoes, which allowed horses (faster and more efficient than oxen) to pull plows; and a shift from a two-field to a three-field system of crop rotation.[4]

Many scholars disagree with White's thesis of an agricultural revolution. Historian of agriculture Karl Brunner noted that the renewed study of archaeo-logical finds (particularly an important find of fifth-century tools and implements at Osterburken in Germany) and the reexamination of objects in museums sup-port a view of gradual technological change in agricultural implements from Roman to early medieval times. Indeed, transitional kinds of plowshares that anticipated the heavy medieval plow have been found from late imperial Rome. With regard to scythes, long-handled cutting implements used for harvesting (Figure 18), Brunner suggested the same gradual development. When harvest-ing hay, a peasant swung the scythe, cutting a number of stalks with a single swing. But for much of the medieval era, peasants cut grain with a sickle (Figure 19), one sheaf at a time, to avoid losing any of the crop. Scholars disagree about when the scythe began to be used for harvesting grain. Michael Toch suggested a much later date than proponents of a revolutionary hypothesis have assumed, even as late as the sixteenth century. He argued that agricultural productivity in the early middle ages increased, not by virtue of technological change, but by "the more intensive application of human work" and by "diffusion, organisational adaptation and elaboration." Recently, Georges Raepsaet and Georges Comet have emphasized the complexity of technological change in agriculture and the importance of the social context to such change.[5]

Whatever the rate of long-term change, the work of the peasants involved an exacting and largely unchanging routine. They plowed in the spring, sowed seeds by hand, and then smoothed the soil by dragging brushwood over it, or, later, with a wooden harrow. In the summer, fields had to be weeded and manured. Sheep and other livestock had to be tended, gardens cultivated, hay cut and stored. In the fall, grain was harvested, threshed, and stored. Winter was the season for repairing tools and making clothing. Each household would have several fruit trees, perhaps a small vegetable garden, and some animals, usually sheep and pigs,

Figure 18. *Peasant sharpening the blade of his scythe for mowing hay. Jamb of the Door of the Virgin, west front of the Cathedral of Notre Dame, Paris, 1210–20. Photo credit: Steven A. Walton.*

less often cattle. The village maintained a common pasture where animals could graze, and woods where pigs could root and where firewood, nuts, and berries could be gathered. A system prevailed wherein villagers plowed, sowed, and harvested crops together while a herdsman watched the animals in the pasture. Village women made simple clothing. Villagers often lived in mud huts with thatched roofs; they ate mostly bread and drank wine or ale. Meat was scarce, but was sometimes available after the slaughter of a pig, a tough animal that could fend for itself by rooting. Pork was preserved by salting, while pigskin was used to make shoes, harnesses, belts, and bags.[6]

There is little doubt that agricultural productivity began to increase in the tenth century. Scholars have argued that changes were gradual, and that the causes of an increased food supply are a complex matter—for example, the decline in violence during the century after the worst period of raids by Vikings and other marauders, and also a small but significant warming of the climate. Rather than endorsing a technologically driven model of agricultural revolution, historians now take a comparative view. They ask what motivated one region to adopt technological changes while neighboring regions did not. They ask about the connections between rural and urban areas, agriculture and trade, connections

Figure 19. *Peasant cutting grain with a sickle. Drawing from Herrad of Landsberg,* Hortus deliciarum, *twelfth century (original destroyed). From* **Das Lustgärtlein der Herrad von Landsberg,** *ed. Maria Heinsius (Kolmar im Elass: Alsatia Verlag, n.d.), plate 21.*

that have been investigated especially in the Low Countries (present-day Netherlands and Belgium). Such questions signal a shift toward a conception of medieval agriculture as part of market economy rather than as a subsistence economy, particularly after the eleventh century.[7]

Whatever the other causes may be, the rising productivity of medieval agriculture can be attributed at least in part to improvements in agricultural technique. Very gradually, beginning in the eighth century, peasants changed from a two-field system of crop rotation to a three-field system. This new system emerged primarily in the north because it required spring planting, successful only in regions of wet soil. Available land would be divided into three parts. One-third lay fallow and one-third was planted in the fall with winter crops such as wheat and rye that would be harvested in the summer. The third part was planted in the spring with oats, barley, or nitrogen-fixing legumes. This could increase crop productivity by fully a third. But the changeover seems to have occurred far later than had once been assumed; one historian writes that "not until the mid-thirteenth century do we find a conscious and regular rotation." And rotation always varied according to region, soil, climate, demand, and custom.[8]

There were innovations that resulted in the more efficient use of animal power, in particular the harnessing of horses as draft animals after the invention of a rigid horse collar. The traditional view was that the Romans had used a horse harness that put pressure on the windpipe, choking it when it tried to pull heavy loads. Although this view has been challenged as overly simplistic, it is nevertheless true that the rigid horse collar was a new medieval development. It rested on the animal's collarbone, allowing it to use its entire bodyweight to draw the load while at the same time breathing freely. While the rigid horse collar may have been invented in central Asia, it came into widespread European use after the tenth century. Another type of improved harnassing called the breast strap harness, which originated in ancient China, was also widely adopted in medieval Europe, especially in southern regions. Other improvements included the use of horseshoes, which helped to prevent lameness, and harnesses whereby horses could be hitched in tandem (one in front of the other) rather than side by side. Unlike oxen, horses require grain, such as oats, in addition to hay. Even though they are faster than oxen and have greater endurance, their employment as a draft animal was a gradual process, never universal, and varied from one region to another. In Flanders, for example, the horse was widely used from the twelfth century on, but this was "much more precocious use" than in regions such as Picardy in northern France, or England, where the-ox-to-horse transition did not occur until the sixteenth century.[9]

In some areas, especially where dispersed settlements predominated, peasants cultivated their own land, called *allods*, and could consume all the products of their labor. In much of the rest of Europe, however, villages came to be ruled by lords in accord with a system called manorialism. While the origins of this system are controversial, it seems to have been generally in place by Carolingian times in the early ninth century. The land controlled by the lord, including one or more villages, was called a manor. Conditions and terms varied widely from one region to another, and even from one manor to another. Lords gained control of villages in a variety of ways, perhaps because of the peasants' need for protection from marauders, or simply by virtue of the disproportionate power of the lord. The lord and lady might live in the manor house with their children and supervise the peasants themselves, or they could employ a bailiff or overseer who supervised the work and collected the lord's revenues. Usually the lord took from a third to half of the produce, as well as livestock and fish caught in his streams. The lord's holdings, including the strips of the fields that belonged to him, were called the *desmesne*. His animals grazed on the common pasture. Male peasants supplied labor for building and digging ditches, while peasant women, supervised by the lady of the manor, often worked in the manor house spinning, weaving, and performing other chores.[10]

Most of the tools, equipment, and food used by both lord and peasant were made on the manor or in the village. Flour had to be ground from grain, bread baked, beer, wine, cheese, and butter prepared by various methods. Animals had to be slaughtered and meat cured and made into sausages. If the laws of the manor allowed, peasants fished. From the forest, fruit and berries had to be gathered along with wood for fuel and other purposes such as making tools, barrels, and furniture. Peasants carried out their burdensome tasks cooperatively, but often divided according to gender. While men did most heavy plowing and other heavy labor, women and older children may have goaded the oxen. Women bore and cared for children, raised poultry and livestock, milked cows, sheep, and goats, sheared sheep, tended cottage gardens, fetched water from wells, took grain to the mill, gathered firewood, and tended the fire. They spun yarn, made cloth from wool and from fibrous plants, sewed up clothing, did laundry, and prepared food and drink such as ale. In the fields they hoed, weeded, reaped, and tied hay into sheaves. At the end of the harvest, they gleaned, the backbreaking task of picking up stray grains from the field.[11]

As the population increased, more and more land was cleared for cultivation, a process that medieval documents call *assarting*. First brush and light woods were cleared, then heavier forests cut and the troublesome tree roots removed. Marshland was drained as well, a difficult task but one which yielded rich, arable land for cultivation. Land reclamation was a gradual process that is largely undocumented, but is evident from place-names (*assart*, meaning clearing, is found in the names of many new villages), and from other scattered sources. The methods used to expand arable land depended in part upon geography. A special case is the Netherlands, where an extensive system of dikes was built between the twelfth and fourteenth centuries. At the same time, peat moors were drained and made suitable for cultivation by digging parallel ditches, burning the scrub, and then planting crops in the peat. Drainage was maintained only by scrupulous water management.[12]

The emphasis that historians traditionally have placed on cultivation should not obscure the economic significance of uncultivated areas. Paolo Squatriti has noted the growing import of wetlands on the early medieval Italian peninsula. As populations declined and Roman systems of hydraulic management disappeared, marshland was increasingly utilized to obtain "fish, waterfowl, wood, twine, reeds, and pasture, as well as numerous mammals." Occasionally, fishing became a full-time occupation. In the tenth century, for example, the fishers of Pavia on the Po River in northern Italy maintained a fleet of at least sixty boats which they used to reach fisheries. This points to a highly developed enterprise of inland freshwater fishing.[13]

Any generalized picture of medieval agriculture will be modified and vastly complicated by detailed investigation. Regional trends that have been observed include the transition from manorial system to lease-holding—a system in which the peasant simply leases a small plot from the lord—evident in the first half of the twelfth century in Flanders; the continued wage labor performed by peasants to supplement their income; and the increasingly close relationship of large and small farms "bound by the market." Careful studies of agriculture in Denmark and Sweden underscore the diversity between regions and among geographic areas within larger regions. Such studies enhance our sense of the complexity of medieval agriculture, and have ended the dubious practice of investigating one discrete region and then generalizing to all the rest of Europe.[14]

An alternative agricultural system is exemplified by Cistercian farming begun in the twelfth century. The Cistercians were a reformed monastic order founded in Citeaux in southern France. Historians at one time credited the new order with pioneering land clearance and drainage in the twelfth and thirteenth centuries, and there is no doubt that they prospered on their new agricultural estates, called granges. More recent research has shown, however, that Cistercian successes were not the result of clearing land but rather of purchasing already cultivated land, thereby consolidating fragmented acreage and instituting new managerial practices. One of these practices entailed a new form of labor. The Cistercians took on able-bodied peasants as *conversi*, lay brothers who were celibate and entered the monastery as farm laborers. By becoming *conversi*, peasants gained their freedom from obligations to lords, avoided family responsibilities, and found economic security as well as a new religious vocation. The Cistercians recruited *conversi* primarily from the former tenants whose land they had acquired. Cistercian monks also became skilled at obtaining exemptions from obligations to lords, from customary tithes to the church, and from other fees and tolls. In the early decades of the new order, the monks themselves worked along-side the *conversi* and hired day laborers as well. They could move workers from one grange to another as needed. The result was a successful system of agriculture very different from both manorial cultivation and the farming of the free peasant.[15]

In addition to the cultivation of fields, the Cistercians acquired much pastureland and they raised livestock, oxen, horses, cows, and especially sheep. They profited from trends that favored producers of animal products during the twelfth and thirteenth centuries, when the growth of towns created markets for leather, woolens, and parchment, as well as cheese, butter, and meat. In addition to acquiring pasture rights, the Cistercians instituted the practice of transhumance—moving their animals to the mountains in the summer and back to the plains in the winter. This practice was well established in southern France by the twelfth century, but the Cistercians practiced it on a much larger scale which enabled them to maintain herds of hundreds or even thousands of animals.[16]

THE MEDIEVAL MILL

The most important sources of power during the medieval centuries were human and animal muscle power. Yet, machines that harnessed the power of wind and water were also significant. The most important of these machines was the mill, first of all the grist mill for grinding grain into flour for making bread, and for grinding malted grains for making ale and beer. Various types of mills, including those powered by animals and humans, were used by the Romans and continued in use with regional variations during the medieval centuries. The ancients had also used water-powered mills. A magisterial essay by Marc Bloch, published in 1935, insured that the medieval watermill long would remain a focus for historians of technology. Bloch argued that the Romans failed to fully exploit water-powered mills because slaves could grind grain

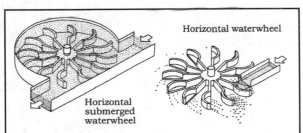

Figure 20. *Horizontal water wheels, from "Pictorial Glossary" in* **The Various and Ingenious Machines of Agostino Ramelli: A Classic Sixteenth-Century Illustrated Treatise on Technology**, *trans. by Martha Teach Gnudi; annotations by Eugene S. Ferguson (1976; reprint, New York: Dover Publications, 1987), 561. Courtesy Dover Publications.*

45

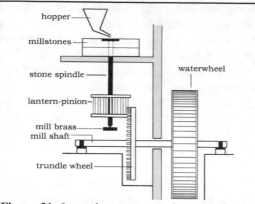

Figure 21. *Internal components of a vertical water mill. The vertical wheel was fed by a system of dams, sluices, and channels. It is attached to a horizontal axle which in turn is attached to a set of gears that turns a vertical axle that turns one of the millstones. From Richard Holt,* **The Mills of Medieval England** *(Oxford: Basil Blackwell, 1988), 118. Courtesy Richard Holt.*

by hand. Historians such as Lynn White Jr. and Jean Gimpel posited an "industrial revolution" in medieval Europe based primarily on their acceptance of Bloch's view that the Romans neglected to exploit water-power, whereas medieval peoples embraced it, especially in the form of powerful mills driven by overshot and under-shot waterwheels. More recently, this idea has been challenged, and it now appears that the Romans exploited waterpower to a greater extent than had been recognized, while medieval use developed very slowly in some areas.[17]

The water-powered mill had a number of variations. Whether and how a particular type was used depended on geography as well as social organization and local custom. The simplest water-powered mill had a horizontal wheel that lay in a stream or river, or else was turned by water flowing from a millrace or funnel (Figure 20.) At the center of the wheel was a vertical shaft that went through a fixed millstone and turned a second millstone. Grain poured into a funnel or hopper fell between the two stones. As the waterwheel turned, the shaft and upper millstone also turned. The grain, crushed between the millstones, emerged from the edges. Vertical water-wheels were more powerful than most horizontal wheels. Yet their gearing made them more compli-cated and expensive (Figure 21). In undershot mills, the water runs underneath the wheel, while in the overshot type the water pours over the top (Figure 22). Some vertical mills were mounted on barges floating in rivers,

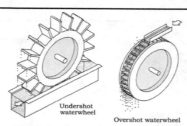

Figure 22. *Undershot and overshot water wheels, from "Pictorial Glossary" in* **The Various and Ingenious Machines of Agostino Ramelli: A Classic Sixteenth-Century Illustrated Treatise on Technology**, *trans. by Martha Teach Gnudi; annotations by Eugene S. Ferguson (1976; reprint, New York: Dover Publications, 1987), 561. Courtesy Dover Publications.*

46

and mills were also mounted on the piers of bridges. In a very different type of mill, common on the Iberian peninsula, water was delivered under pressure, or "powered up." One such type was the tank or *arubah* mill (Figure 23), another the ramp mill (Figure 24). These powerful mills were sometimes used to turn multiple millstones.[18]

Free peasants working their own land might use hand mills or querns and horse mills to grind grain. If they used a watermill, it would most likely be horizontal. On the manor, lords constructed heavier overshot or undershot vertical grist mills and forced peasants to have their grain ground for a fee amounting to a certain proportion of the flour. Because vertical mills were dependent on a reliable water flow, they were more prevalent in some areas than others. The rivers in parts of Italy, prone to floods in the winter and slack water in the summer, were not particularly suitable for vertical waterwheels. John Muendel has investigated archival documents, such as those pertaining to rentals, which mention parts of mills. He concludes that in the north Italian town of Pistoia most if not all watermills were horizontal. But in Florence, his investigations revealed a variety of types of mills, including horizontal, overshot, hybrid horizontal with gearing, floating, and undershot. Paolo Squatriti pointed out that manorial mills prevalent in Francia were not at all characteristic of the Italian peninsula, where urban control of mills and private control by individual peasants was more characteristic. He also

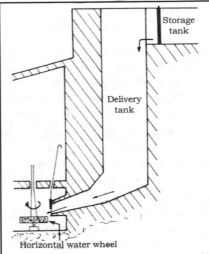

Figure 23. *A tank or arubah-style mill. This mill was constructed with a water tower drained by a pipe and nozzle directed at the paddles of the horizontal wheel. Because it conserved water in its tower, this type of mill was favored in regions of scarce or uneven rainfall, such as the Iberian Peninsula. Courtesy Thomas F. Glick.*

demonstrated the diversity of types of mills in early medieval Italy, where querns and donkey mills existed alongside watermills.[19]

Knowledge of medieval milling has been furthered by archeological investigations. For example, in his description of the archeology of English mills, David Crossley pointed to a new emphasis on the study of complete mill complexes, rather than just the remains of the mill itself. The study of mill-sites now entails investigation of watercourses, weirs, dams, and millponds, as well as the surrounding landscape, which may include surveys of entire valleys.[20]

The post windmill was a medieval invention that appeared in northern Europe and England not long before 1185; Richard Holt called this "the most characteristic contribution of the age to the technology of exploiting natural power, and by far the most important" (Figure 25). While Lynn White Jr. hailed the windmill as crucial to the technological dynamism of medieval Europe, Holt in contrast used the English case to argue that it was a new machine that was used primarily where conditions did not favor the watermill, and that it was adopted rather slowly.[21]

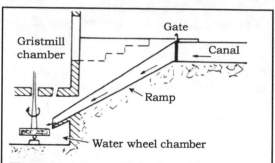

Figure 24. *A ramp mill. In this mill the water was directed onto the paddles of the horizontal wheel from a ramp or canal. This type of mill depends on a continuous flow of water. Courtesy Thomas F. Glick.*

Although grinding grain was by far the most important use, medieval mills were developed for other purposes as well. They were used for sawing wood and for grinding the bark used to tan leather. Water-powered forges were used to hammer the "bloom" in the process of working iron. Mills were used for grinding and sharpening the blades of tools and weapons. Most important, fulling mills were used in the stage of wool cloth-making that involved washing, soaking, and beating by means of hammers. Fulling mills featured the first European appearance of the cam, an eccentric lever that caught the hammer and lifted it, whereupon it would fall onto the cloth from its own weight.[22]

THE MEDIEVAL CASTLE

While village and field were traditional sites for the life and work of the peasant, the life of the nobility came to be centered on the castle. Nobles constructed these massive structures beginning in the ninth and tenth centuries, first as protection during the invasions of the Vikings, Magyars, and Slavic peoples. Later, castles evolved into multipurpose structures that served not only as protection but as residences for noble families, garrisons for feudal armies, administrative centers, and centers of craft production. They became more elaborate as time went on. Beginning as a simple protective enclosure made of earth and wood, and known as the motte-and-bailey castle (Figure 26), they became elaborate stone structures that symbolized the power of the nobles who used them both to defend the surrounding population and to control it.[23]

The motte was an earthen mound topped by a wooden fortification and surrounded by a deep ditch. The bailey consisted of an enclosed yard built outside the ditch encircling the motte. During construction, earth from the ditch would be thrown into the center to create the mound. Then a wooden structure was built on top, sometimes just a tower to house soldiers, but, as time went on, more elaborate structures. Larger residential mottes housed the family and its retainers. The bailey was surrounded by a fence or palisade, usually constructed out of logs. Sometimes a ditch was dug around the bailey as well, which could provide refuge for the noble's horses and cattle, or for villagers living nearby. The ditch between the bailey and motte was crossed by one or more bridges which could be drawn up or destroyed in order to protect those inside from attackers.[24]

The use of the motte-and-bailey castle as an instrument, not of defense, but of subjugation can be seen most clearly in England. In 1066 William and his army of Norman knights crossed the English Channel and defeated the Saxon army in the Battle of Hastings. After his victory William found it difficult to control the rebellious population, so he began entrusting his barons with the construction of castles at crucial defensive points and gave jurisdiction to each of these barons over the surrounding countryside. At the same time he also maintained control, because no baron could build a castle without his permission. By the time of William's death in 1087, there were more than 500 motte-and-bailey castles in England. The Normans were there to stay.[25]

Gradually, beginning in the late tenth century, stone castles replaced motte-and-bailey structures. Although specific origins are controversial, within a hundred years they dotted the European countryside (Figure 27), many of them constructed on motte-and-bailey sites. They consisted originally of a stone tower, meant to garrison troops, that was surrounded by massive stone walls. As uses multiplied beyond mere fortification, castles became more and more elaborate, eventually becoming residences for noble families as well as administrative centers. The most important characteristic of castles were their walls—as much as six meters thick at the base—constructed by making two parallel walls out of ashlar blocks and filling the space with stone rubble. Castles usually incorporated immense towers as well as courtyards and rooms that housed family members, visitors, troops, and supplies.[26]

Figure 25. *A fourteenth-century post windmill. This entire structure rested on a single post and could be turned so that the sails faced the wind. British Library Stowe Ms. 17, f. 89 v. By permission of the British Library.*

In an influential study devoted to Lazio (the area around Rome in central Italy), Pierre Toubert investigated castle building as a phenomenon that was accompanied by changing patterns of social organization and settlement during the eleventh century. This process, which he called *incastellamento*, is the key structural element in a change of settlement patterns associated with the rise of feudalism. Toubert found that bishops and abbeys were important contributors to this movement. Dispersed habitats disappeared, while villages were formed near castles. The purpose of these castles was to dominate the countryside rather than protect it. Archaeologists working in the Iberian Peninsula, most importantly Pierre Guichard, have extended this investigation of *incastellamento*, focusing on its development in both Christian and Arab/Berber areas. Thomas Glick emphasized that the domination of a lord over the surrounding countryside could take a number of different forms. The lord could take rent in kind from peasants in a traditional manorial arrangement, for example, or he could extract taxes.[27]

THE GROWTH OF TOWNS

Although life in the early Middle Ages was overwhelmingly rural, in some areas—especially northern Italy and southern France—remnants of Roman towns remained in greatly diminished form. Whether medieval towns were a development from Roman antecedents or were entirely new is a question that must be decided on a town-by-town basis. In general, however, towns in northern Italy and southern France were more likely to have had a Roman core than those that grew up in regions further from the center of the ancient empire. Remnants of Roman times included physical structures—walls, ruined buildings, and materials such as bricks and stones which medieval people often used to build new, more humble, structures. The study of towns, including their decline and subsequent medieval growth, has been substantially advanced by archaeological investigation of individual sites.[28]

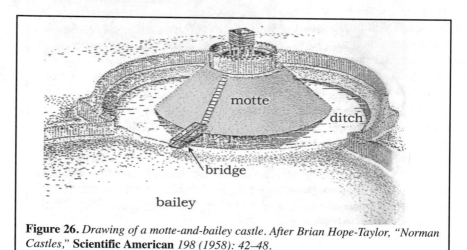

Figure 26. *Drawing of a motte-and-bailey castle. After Brian Hope-Taylor, "Norman Castles,"* **Scientific American** *198 (1958): 42–48.*

The specific origins of medieval towns usually involved a variety of factors. In part they grew up in response to increased trade and commerce. Occasionally they were created as marketing centers by powerful lords. They could develop around a monastery or the palace of a bishop, or near a lord's castle or a river crossing or trading post. In the eleventh century, kings and bishops began giving charters to towns, guaranteeing them a significant degree of autonomy and freedom. Whatever their origins, towns became a dynamic focus of medieval life after the eleventh century.[29]

The effects of the revival of long-distance trade on urbanization deserves particular emphasis. Michael McCormick's monumental study of the "European economy" made it clear that the volume of travel and trade in the Carolingian Age between 700 and 900 was far greater than previously has been supposed. Travelers' destinations included numerous small ports as well as those on major trade routes. Venice, on the Adriatic Sea, developed an important trade with Constantinople; wheat, lumber, salt, and wine were shipped to the Byzantine capital in return for silk and spices. In the north, England began sending tin and raw wool to the European continent, bringing back Flemish wool cloth, silver from German lands, and luxury goods from northern Italy. In the early twelfth century, the counts of Champagne staged great trade fairs, providing security and safe roads for merchants from north and south. Fairs were also established in Lombardy, and the towns of Flanders traded their famous wool cloth for numerous other commodities.

Figure 27. *Harlech Castle, Gwynedd, North Wales, built 1283–86. Photo credit: Pamela O. Long.*

The Vikings gradually changed from marauders to traders who brought furs and slaves down the coast to French and German lands and down the Russian rivers to Constantinople, purchasing armor, gold, and silver. The Crusades, undertaken by western knights and merchants to capture the lands of the so-called infidel, boosted this long-distance trade; for example, when the First Crusade of 1097 resulted in the creation of the Latin Kingdom of Jerusalem, trade to the eastern Mediterranean expanded greatly. Four developments were intrinsically related: the growth of long-distance trade, the great expansion of the use of money, the proliferation of specialized crafts based in the new towns, and urbanization itself.[30]

Cities were magnets for trade, but they also became centers of manufacture for everyday wares and luxuries, for saddles, pots and pans, glassware, jewelry, gloves, and consumables, most importantly bread. In the thirteenth century the most significant manufacture in western Europe was woolen cloth. And, as Steven Epstein noted, "perhaps the most distinctive, and relatively recent, feature of urban society was the large number of people who supported themselves through wage labour." Most cities were composed of neighborhoods, sometimes organized along craft lines. Usually, "dirty" trades that polluted the water or produced disagreeable smells—butchers, tanners, cloth fullers—were located at the edge of town. Many crafts were organized into guilds after the twelfth century. Boys and sometimes girls were apprenticed to masters in workshops. After some years, apprentices became journeymen or day laborers and were authorized to work for wages. Some journeymen became masters, setting up shops of their own. Guilds governed the rules of apprenticeship, set standards for the quality of the goods produced, and prevented outsiders from producing those goods. They also served social functions, burying deceased members, caring for indigent widows and children. Many scholars no longer accept the traditional generalization that guilds represented a conservative force, inhibiting invention and innovation. S. R. Epstein argues that the transmission of technologies throughout Europe was greatly facilitated by journeymen traveling from one town to another to get work (tramping), a well-established practice followed by many young artisans.[31]

CRAFTS AND TRADES

In the early medieval village and manor, many material objects were made on site. Peasants made shoes, bags, and harnesses from pigskin; they fabricated wool or flax cloth and clothing; and they made wooden farm tools and cooking implements. The small amount of iron used for tools was mined elsewhere and worked by smiths, who at first constructed their forges and anvils in the forests to be near the necessary fuel. Eventually, however, the smith became a valued artisan in the village and manor, making horseshoes, plowshares, pots, pans, armor, and weaponry.[32]

Another important site of early medieval craft production was the monastery. Many everyday items used by monks and nuns were made in monastic workshops, including wooden objects such as furniture and barrels, cloth and clothing, pottery, leather goods, and metal objects made by the smith. Some monasteries also supported skilled artisans who produced finely worked liturgical objects, from candlesticks to embroidered garments. This specialized work is vivid in the pseudonymous twelfth-century treatise, *De diversis artibus* (On Diverse Arts) by Theophilus ("Lover of God"). The author was probably Benedictine monk Roger of Helmarshausen, whose metalwork is known from three highly decorated objects—a jewel-studded book cover in Nuremberg and two portable altars in the cathedral treasury of Paderborn. In addition to providing numerous craft recipes on painting, glass, and metalwork, Theophilus discussed the ethics of monastic craftsmanship, stressing the importance of virtue, humility, piety, faith, and the open sharing with others of God-given craft skill and knowledge.[33]

The growth of towns was characterized by the proliferation of specialized crafts. Tanners made leather out of skins which they provided to glovers, saddle-makers, and artisans who made parchment for books. Textile workers produced cloth, wool, linen, cotton, and silk. Metalworkers included goldsmiths, silversmiths, ironworkers, armorers, and smiths who worked with copper, tin, and pewter. Medieval crafts included glassmaking for vessels and windows, pottery and tile-making, painting, sculpting, and brick-making. Carpenters and joiners specialized in making a variety of objects from barrels to marriage chests to altarpieces.[34]

The manufacture of wool cloth was the most important medieval industry. Most stages of production were carried out by specialists: shearing sheep and cleaning the wool, combing and carding, spinning, putting the yarn on the loom, weaving, dyeing, fulling, finishing. Wool cloth manufacture changed significantly over time. Early medieval cloth-making was a local, family or manor-based craft, carried out for the most part by women. Spinning was done by hand and cloth was woven on vertical warp-weighted looms (Figure 28). During the eleventh and twelfth centuries, wool became important in long-distance trade, and wool manufacture developed as a significant industry in many towns, especially in northern Italy and Flanders. Horizontal looms replaced vertical looms (Figure 29). The spinning wheel, introduced in the thirteenth century, was improved with foot treadles and a mechanism to control the tension. As textile manufacture changed from a local craft industry to one that produced commodities for long-distance trade, labor and power relationships changed. Women remained involved in spinning and other tasks within a "putting out" system in their own homes, and were paid (very poorly) by the piece. Most other parts of the process fell to the control of men, especially the drapers or wool merchants. The industry became organized into four major crafts: weaving, fulling, dyeing, and finishing.[35]

Figure 28. *Vertical two-beam loom from a twelfth-century copy of the Utrecht Psalter. Trinity College, Cambridge, Ms. R17,1, f. 263. Courtesy Trinity College, Cambridge.*

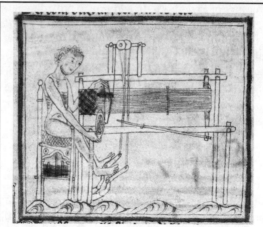

Figure 29. *Horizontal loom, c. 1250. Trinity College, Cambridge, Ms. 0.9.34, f. 34 v. Courtesy Trinity College, Cambridge.*

ARCHITECTURE AND BUILDING CONSTRUCTION

The architectural styles such as the Romanesque that emerged in the late tenth century and the Gothic that developed in the twelfth each entailed specific building techniques. All building construction, from humble to monumental, required the acquisition or fabrication of materials such as brick, stone, and wood, and their subsequent working by means of specialized tools and techniques (Figure 30). Aside from stone castles and great abbeys, the most prominent structures on the medieval landscape were churches and cathedrals. The new Romanesque style was seen mostly in cathedrals but also in other buildings such as abbeys. This style displayed a new interest in articulating and clarifying space. Elements such as side chapels were carefully integrated into the design as a whole. The creators of Romanesque buildings aimed to make coherent and unified

Figure 30. *Building the Tower of Babel. Drawing from Herrad of Landsberg,* Hortus deliciarum, *twelfth century (original destroyed). Equipment seen here includes a hoe, at left; a hod (second figure from left) for carrying mortar; a pick, chisel, and mallet used by the stone-cutters on the right; a plumbline held by the man on top; and a mason's trowel and mason's square held by the man standing at right-center. From* **Das Lustgärtlein der Herrad von Landsberg**, *ed. Maria Heinsius (Kolmar im Elass: Alsatia Verlag, n.d.), plate 7.*

spaces. This interest in articulating space led to the development of particular motifs, for example, a system of alternating columns and piers to divide and support a long wall (typical of central European Romanesque buildings) or a motif created by the Normans, the separation of one bay from another by tall shafts running from the floor to the ceiling. A further innovation, first achieved in Durham Cathedral in England, was to create a rib vault (an arched ceil-

Figure 31. *Central nave of Durham Cathedral with rib-vaulted ceiling. Photo credit: Scala/Art Resource, New York.*

ing with sections separated by projecting bands or ribs) over the wide nave or center aisle of the church (Figure 31). At Durham the interest in articulation led to a technological innovation that would become intrinsic to a new style, the Gothic.[36]

The Gothic cathedral may be traced to the mid-twelfth century and the new choir of St. Denis Abbey near Paris, built between 1140 and 1144. Three technical features accompanied the development of this new style—the pointed arch, the rib vault, and the flying buttress—each of which had developed separately in previous centuries. The flying buttress on the outside took the weight of the vaulting and the roof, enabling masons to build thin, high walls, filled with stained glass (Figure 32). As a result, Gothic buildings seem to soar and on bright days are flooded with light. Scholars continue to study these great structures, sometimes with new methodologies. Robert Mark has used the methods of structural engineering, creating plastic models and subjecting them to various stresses, in order to analyze how the cathedrals work as structures. He discovered, for example, that the pinnacles resting on the top of the buttresses of Rheims are not merely decorative but add to stability.[37] (See Figure 33.)

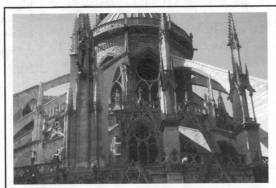

Figure 32. *Notre Dame Cathedral, Paris (1163–1345), in a view facing the apse of the flying buttresses. Photo credit: Steven A. Walton.*

Of course, medieval masons did not have recourse to modern methods of structural analysis. Rather, they learned their craft by apprenticeship and thus acquired knowledge of previous construction. They built cathedrals bay-by-bay. Mark suggested that they tested a new idea on the first completed bay and, if it worked, carried it out in the succeeding bays. They experimented, he suggested, "by observing cracks developing in the tension-sensitive lime mortar used to cement the cut stones, and then by modifying the form of the structure in order to expunge the cracking." Designing the building as a whole, masons used "constructive geometry" in which they manipulated geometric forms, using drawing tools such as the straightedge and dividers, to determine the overall dimensions of ground plans, facades, and all the various elements of the building. When construction began, a "great measure" would be established to create the ground plan, and would then be employed throughout the construction. As Lon Shelby explained, the methods of the masons were traditional, empirical, and experimental. The great measure was part of the building. Once the dimension of one element had been fixed, all the other elements were "expressed in terms of the first." The unit of measure became a module for the entire building.[38]

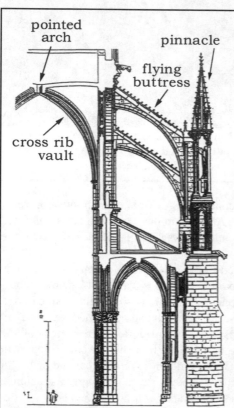

Figure 33. *Pinnacle, buttresses, and cross-rib vault of Reims Cathedral. From Eugène-Emmanuel Violet-Le-Duc,* **Dictionnaire raisonné de l'architecture française du XI e au XVIe siècle**, *10 vols. (Paris: B. Bance, 1858–68), article "Cathédrale," vol. 4, page 318, fig. 14.*

The master mason was in charge of both the design and construction, and usually stayed on-site during the construction process. He worked closely with a patron, and with masons, journeymen, and apprentices. He supervised construction involving stone and brick, but not that involving wood, glass, or lead, which were in the charge of carpenters, glaziers, and plumbers. The mason was actually concerned with three sites—the quarry where the stone was obtained; the lodge, a wooden building which served as his workshop; and the building site itself. Stone was hewn from the quarry and brought to the lodge where it was precisely cut according to where it was to be placed. To shape stones exactly, masons used numerous templates for piers, columns, vaults, doorways, and windows.[39]

Masons were paid wages. Usually, they were not organized as urban guilds, because they traveled to worksites that could be in the countryside and or in distant towns. Some master masons became building contractors and supplemented their wages by profits acquired by supplying lumber, stone, or other materials. The lodge, usually constructed near the building site, functioned as the workshop of the masons and also as their organizational center.[40]

THE VALUE OF WORK

Scholars have argued that labor, including manual labor and skilled craftwork, gained more status in the medieval centuries than in the ancient world. And there is indeed much evidence for the ancient contempt for handwork, which was associated with slavery. Yet, recent scholarship has pointed to the positive ancient traditions alongside the negative. In the early medieval centuries, the growth of monasticism encouraged the appreciation of work. Monastic regulations treated labor as an essential part of the life of piety. In a different context, the growth of commerce and of towns led to an increase of skilled artisans and an increased appreciation for their skill and their wares. The emergence of merchant and craft guilds provided means of regulating particular trades, including rules for apprenticeship and quality control, but they also offered peer companionship and support for members, including funeral expenses for indigent members and support of indigent widows and their children.[41]

With the growth of learning, the proliferation of schools, and the establishment of universities in the twelfth and thirteenth centuries, the "mechanical arts," as skilled craftwork was called, were sometimes included alongside the "liberal arts" in accounts of the disciplines. (The seven liberal arts comprised the trivium: grammar, rhetoric, and dialectic or logic, and the quadrivium, geometry, arithmetic, music, and astronomy.) Particularly notable was the *Didascalicon* of Hugh of St. Victor (c. 1096–1141) who gave seven mechanical arts—fabric-making, armament, commerce, agriculture, hunting, medicine, and theatrics—an important place. Nevertheless, during the medieval centuries, the skilled trades remained separate from the learned disciplines. The latter were communicated entirely in the language of learning, Latin. The medieval universities, first created in the early thirteenth century, admitted only men and all lectures and discussion, all books, were in Latin. In contrast, skilled artisans learned their trade within apprenticeship arrangements, and they did not learn Latin. The closing of the gap between the learned and the skilled, and interchange between the two groups occurred only in later centuries, beginning in the fifteenth and sixteenth.[42]

Although work was often divided by gender, women participated in numerous productive activities and even controlled some of them. David Herlihy has investigated the evidence for a trend in which female work in public arenas was gradually curtailed in the late medieval and early modern centuries. In the early medieval centuries, however, women produced virtually all cloth and clothing.

In the manor house and sometimes in monasteries, they worked in a workroom called the *gynaeceum*. Women are praised as fabric workers from the Carolingian age to the thirteenth century. Female participation in cloth-making cut across class lines. Noblewomen occupied supervisory roles and young girls, whether rich or poor, were often taught to spin and sew. From the eleventh century on, women gradually appear less frequently in the documentary evidence for cloth-making, while men appear more frequently. By the thirteenth century men and women were working side-by-side in an industry once dominated by women. Their lack of legal autonomy and their exclusion from developing forms of credit prevented women from effectively engaging in long distance trade, while the growing importance of male ascetic monastic culture effectively excluded them, as David Noble has argued, from numerous other domains.[43]

Work in a particular city, Paris, is illuminated by seven tax rolls from the late thirteenth and early fourteenth centuries (1292–1313) and by a copy of the principal guild statutes from the same period. The tax was called the *taille* and the tax rolls called the *Books of the Taille of the City of Paris*. It shows that women worked in 172 occupations in 1292 while men worked in 325. In 1313 women appear in 130 occupations and men in 276. Women appear "as drapers, money changers, jewelers, and mercers." Female mint workers, copyists, tavern-keepers, masons, artists, shoemakers, girdle makers, smiths, shield makers, archers, and candle makers are also found. That women dominated the silk cloth industry is evident in the records of female silk guilds. Only a very few occupations involving long-distance travel and heavy hauling were exclusively male. The woolen industry, however, was different. In 1292 there were 73 male weavers and only one female (who may actually have been working on silk or linen). In the same year there were 15 male dyers and again only one female. Here is an indication of a change that occurred all over Europe. When wool became important in long-distance commerce, it fell to the control of men. In all occupations, female workers earned about two-thirds as much as males.[44]

There are sources that enable historians to gain some knowledge of women's work in other parts of Europe as well. For example, because ale-making was regulated in England, records survive from rural tribunals or manor courts. Making ale entailed soaking the barley for several days, draining it, germinating it to create malt, drying and grinding the malt, and then adding it to hot water to inculcate fermentation. The wort was drained from this mixture. Herbs and yeast could be added. Equipment for the process included large pots, vats, ladles, and straining cloths. Judith Bennett has shown that during the thirteenth and fourteenth centuries, the production of ale, the primary drink of the peasantry, was carried out entirely by women. When production later became more commercial, men controlled it.[45]

In medieval Montpellier, in southern France, 30 of the 208 apprenticeship contracts extant from before 1350 concern females. Girls were apprenticed as bakers, spinners of gold thread, silver gilders, embroiderers, basket weavers, painters, and tailors; as in many medieval towns, women were extremely active in local retail markets. In Exeter, in southwest England, court records show that women were active in retailing, brewing, candle making, leather working, and cloth manufacture. Family occupation was important in determining the trade of both males and females. In both Montpellier and Exeter, craftswomen sometimes practiced trades similar to those of their fathers and husbands.[46]

* * *

The brief discussion of women's work underscores a methodological issue pertinent to the study of all of medieval history. What can be known is based to a significant degree on written sources, and such sources always derive from one particular locality. The reason a source exists (whether it consists of court records or guild regulations or something similar) influences the nature of the material reported, on the one hand, but, on the other, fails to inform us about the many activities which were not included. The extent to which conclusions from any particular source can be generalized is always an issue. For the medieval centuries such problems are exacerbated by the relative paucity of sources. The development of medieval archeology and the incorporation of its findings by historians have brought about important new sources of information.

Scholars recently have explored particular regions in great detail, while at the same time treating their conclusions comparatively. In the matter of three technologies in particular—technologies pertaining to the military, to transportation, and to communication—the major geographic and political regions treated in this booklet were linked in important ways. Hence the following three chapters will underscore such interrelations topically rather than region by region.

4

WARFARE AND MILITARY TECHNOLOGY

Offensive weaponry and defensive fortifications lie at the heart of any discussion of military technology, yet hardware and fortifications, tactics and strategy, are never separate and distinct from political organization, logistics, and leadership. During the medieval centuries, battles, whether on land or sea, were fought primarily by men. But in the west women could become lords of fiefs, or act as such in the absence of their husbands, and they sometimes acquired military responsibilities as well. In all regions, women could be involved in provisioning armies with food, clothing, and shelter. Apart from that, however, warfare profoundly affected noncombatants, whether they be men, women, or children. Onerous taxes were borne by peasants, and a field that a peasant had just planted could well be ravaged by battle. Crops and vineyards might be destroyed, animals taken away; innocents could be killed, maimed, or forced into a lifetime of slavery.[1]

Warfare was endemic during most of the Middle Ages. Military technologies and organization differed between Byzantium, Islam, and the west, but capabilities were often more-or-less evenly matched. As combatants confronted one another, they sometimes shifted technologies and strategies, adopting the ways of their enemies as their own; hence warfare sometimes functioned as a conduit for the transmission of knowledge, albeit of a destructive sort. As Maurice Keen pointed out, however, Byzantium and the west had opposite trajectories with regard to modes of military organization. In the early medieval centuries, Byzantium was a major territorial power with an efficient system of taxation, an extensive bureaucracy, and a powerful army with a well-established command structure. This army was fully prepared to mobilize at short notice for large-scale campaigns. Yet, by the eleventh century, Byzantine imperial authority was under erosion by the increasing independence of the great landowners in the provinces. In the early medieval west, by contrast, territories were largely controlled by landed nobles who were unconstrained by centralized authority and thus militarily independent. Later, emerging monarchies consolidated their power over the landed aristocracies.[2]

At the time of the emperor Justinian (483–565), Byzantine forces comprised both infantry and cavalry, recruited from Germanic tribes, Huns, Alans, and other peoples of the steppe (the plains of southeastern Europe and western Asia), as well as Greeks and Romans. On the desert borderlands of Syria, the Byzantines allied themselves with nomadic Arab tribes. Arab tribal chiefs, called *phylarchs*, were paid to defend the frontier and were eventually given responsibility for maintaining order in Syria and Palestine; with the advent of Islam, these Arab allies became enemies. In addition to former *phylarchs*, other Arab troops were drawn from settled tribes and from among camel nomads. By the mid-seventh century, a significant portion of the Islamic infantry in Syria was made up of archers of Yemeni origin. To the east, after the Arabs defeated the Sasanian Empire, many Sasanians were enlisted into the army of Islam.[3]

Many centuries before the arrival of Islam, camel nomads had gained control of the trade routes of the Arabian Peninsula, a dominance that Richard Bulliet attributed in part to the development of camel saddles. The ascendance of these nomads and their control of transport required political and economic power. For that, it was necessary to achieve some degree of social integration with the settled communities. This was only possible if they were capable of wielding force, and that was "achieved by the camel-borne warrior mounted upon a north Arabian saddle." The north Arabian saddle was made with two large inverted Vs, one sitting in front of the hump and one behind. The Vs were connected on the sides either by straight or crossed sticks, so that the entire saddle formed a rigid square. The rider sat atop this square, his weight distributed along the ribs of the camel rather than concentrated on the hump. In packing, the load was divided into equal portions and tied to the sides of the camel. The new saddle enabled the nomads to fight effectively while wielding swords and spears. Previous saddles, however useful for packing or simply riding, could not protect a combatant brandishing a weapon from being thrown from his mount when under assault. Bulliet argues that the new saddle did just that and thus must have been invented to solve the problem.[4]

These were ancient, not medieval developments, but they had profound repercussions in the medieval era by rendering nomadic tribes capable of controlling the desert trade. Because a warrior mounted on a camel was always at a disadvantage against an adversary mounted on a horse, these nomads simultaneously bred and developed the Arabian war horse, which facilitated effective combat not only in the desert but in or near settlements protected by mounted horsemen. Together, the camel and the horse enabled the nomads to control the caravan trade across the desert and to become a looming military presence near settlements as well.[5]

Within a few decades during the mid-seventh century, Arab military forces were transformed into a unified Islamic army; they had conquered the Sasanian state and they had wrested vast territories from the Byzantines, including Egypt and Syria. Both the Sasanian and Byzantine empires had been left in a weakened state by internal conflict and conflict with each other. Often at odds with exploitive Byzantine or Sasanian rulers, conquered populations sometimes capitulated to the Muslims after receiving guarantees of life, liberty, the security of property, and the right to practice their own religion. Islamic ruling elites were well-organized and cohesive, and could readily recruit seasoned Arab tribesmen into the ranks of their fighting forces. In Syria, after defeated Byzantines fled, the Arabs occupied their palaces and transformed churches into mosques. The Umayyad caliphs (660–750) established their capital in Damascus and developed a sophisticated administrative structure. Though the mid-seventh-century Islamic army was made up primarily of Arab fighters, increasingly thereafter it incorporated non-Arab troops from conquered territories, most importantly from Berber tribes in Morocco. Some Berbers converted to Islam, some were Jewish, others worshiped pagan gods, but, together, the Berbers led by the Arabs comprised a formidable fighting force.[6]

In the mid-eighth century, the Abbasids overthrew the Umayyads and created a government with a new army whose divisions were based on family and place of origin. The headquarters was the "Round City" of Baghdad where the Caliph's palace commanded a vast garrison for the Islamic state. Under Abbasid rule, the dominant military classes lived in towns and owned land that they leased to peasants. During the ninth century, the Abbasids increasingly used troops who were Mamluks, Turkish slaves mostly purchased from central Asian chiefs who sold their own people, or from parents selling their children. After rigorous training, they would join the army as free men. An archaeological analysis of areas where troops were quartered in Samarra north of Baghdad (where the Abbasids briefly made their capital) indicates that the size of the army grew from 94,300 men in 836 to 156,700 in the 860s. From written sources, we learn that it was organized into units of ten to fifteen men, each of which lived in a four-room house that had a stable for their horses. Other sources suggest a state policy of purchasing wives for the soldiers, so it appears that some troops lived in the cantonments with wives and children. Eventually, with the fragmentation of Abbasid political authority in the tenth century, the Mamluks gained political power for themselves.[7]

Because their loyalty was never considered a certainty, the Mamluks had to be paid well, and this expense led to a shortfall of cash for the central administration. By the mid-ninth century, military personnel were permitted to collect taxes directly, a policy that led to the militarization of the state. Need for revenue also led to the *iqta* system, first instituted in Iraq in the tenth century, wherein military personnel were provided with revenue-producing estates. Soldiers granted an *iqta* had authority to collect taxes from peasants and town dwellers, but did not have jurisdiction over them. A high-level commander might be given a whole province. In effect, this policy amounted to the assignment of tax revenue from a particular place in exchange for military service. It should not be equated with the feudal system of the west wherein a lord gave a vassal a fief in exchange for loyalty and military service; the mutual obligations inherent in feudalism were absent. Rather, *iqta* was a straightforward method of supporting troops.[8]

After the loss of Syria and Egypt to the Arabs, the agrarian center of the Byzantine Empire shifted to Asia Minor (the Asiatic part of present-day Turkey). The Byzantines instituted a new provincial defense system involving *themes* — autonomous military units and the large territorial districts that supported them. *Themes* were headed by generals (*strategoi*) who functioned as both civilian and military governors. The system enabled the Empire to defend itself against Arab and Slav invaders, but also presented a threat from the autonomous *strategoi*. In response, the emperors created a combined army of foot soldiers and cavalry called "the regiments," garrisoned in Constantinople. The Byzantine navy was made up of both imperial and *thematic* elements, and it was this new organization that saved the Byzantine Empire for many centuries.[9]

In contrast to the Byzantine and Islamic states, centralized power was lacking in the early medieval west, as was its accompaniment—relatively large standing armies. In the Barbarian states, free men (sometimes including peasants) were obliged to serve when summoned by the king, and to provide their own supplies and equipment. Laws regarding military service varied somewhat from one kingdom to another. In the seventh century in Francia, the Merovingian monarchy was beset by the growing power of the aristocracy and by conflict and civil wars. The Carolingians before and during the reign of Charlemagne vastly expanded their territories by means of almost yearly military campaigns carried out by forces for the most part newly assembled every year. How many foot soldiers and cavalry were recruited for each campaign is often a matter of debate, but there is no doubt that the early Carolingian monarchs, including Charlemagne himself, were inspired and enthusiastic military leaders.[10]

WEAPONS AND EQUIPMENT

In eastern Mediterranean lands during the seventh and eighth centuries, opposing forces borrowed tactics and technologies from each other. The Byzantines learned much about mounted archery from their nomadic enemies from central Asia, the Huns and the Avars. These skilled archers used a small, powerful weapon called a short bow (Figure 34). It had an inner core of wood, a layer of horn on the side facing the archer, and an outer layer of sinew. Bowstrings were often silk. Byzantine archers did not shoot from moving horses in the manner of the nomads, but they used a variety of finger-draw techniques, as well as the powerful central Asian thumb draw. By the seventh century the Arabs were using these same techniques.[11]

Figure 34. *Rider with a short bow, after an image on a plate made in eastern Iran or central Asia in the eighth or ninth century. Photograph of plate in David Nicolle,* **Medieval Warfare Source Book: Christian Europe and Its Neighbours** *(London: Brockhampton Press, 1998), 53.*

In the west, archers came from the poorer classes, did not ride horses, and used the traditional bow (Figure 35). A very different kind of bow—a bow with a mechanical release mechanism—was the crossbow, a powerful weapon that was gradually improved in the later medieval centuries. Crossbows may have survived from ancient Roman times or they may have been introduced from China in the tenth century, but in continental Europe they eventually became the primary weapon of archers. Some were drawn with a windlass (Figure 36). The crossbow was not widely used in Islamic lands until the twelfth century, but in al-Andalus it came to be preferred. Some crossbows had a stirrup at the end of the stock, into which the archer placed his foot before drawing the string by means of a hook on the end of a rope attached to his belt.[12] (See Figure 37.)

A new kind of bow emerged in the thirteenth century, the longbow; the English first encountered this weapon while fighting the Welsh. Archers drew the string to the ear rather than to the chest, allowing the use of a longer arrow that had a longer range and twice the impact of an arrow shot

Figure 35. *Archer with an ordinary bow, after an image on the Bayeux Tapestry. Photograph of section of tapestry in Jim Bradbury,* **The Medieval Archer** *(New York: St. Martin's Press, 1985), 35.*

from an ordinary bow. The English army quickly adopted the new bow, at first using skilled Welsh and Cheshire archers.[13]

Swords, daggers, spears, javelins, and war axes took different forms. The Byzantines preferred a long-bladed cavalry sword, while Muslim fighters carried the shorter infantry sword. From the Avars, the Byzantines adopted spears equipped with wrist-straps at the center of the shaft. Arab spears had long reed shafts, the best of which came from India and the Persian Gulf. A significant new technology of the early medieval era was the wood-framed horse saddle, which protected the horse's spine by shifting the weight of the rider to each side. This new saddle was only selectively adopted, however; Arab and Berber cavalry rode on padded saddles, at times bareback. By the early seventh century, stirrups were being used throughout the Eurasian steppes.[14]

Byzantine and Muslim soldiers used straight swords, and both used a variety of spears and javelins. The Byzantines had four different kinds of battleaxes, while Muslim cavalry typically carried single-handed "saddle axes." Defensive equipment was diverse. It included shields, helmets, and metallic or soft body armor, the latter made of leather or felt and quilting. Horse armor, too, was either metallic or soft, and could cover the entire animal or protect only the front. The Arabs adopted stirrups from central Asia in the eighth century, though without any immediate influence on tactics.[15]

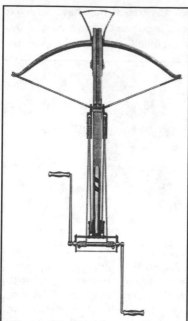

Figure 36. *Crossbow with windlass. From Ralph Payne-Gallwey,* **The Crossbow** *(London: Longmans, Green, 1903), figure 56.*

An important find of English military equipment was discovered by the excavation of Sutton Hoo, a ship burial site of a seventh-century king in East Anglia. The military artifacts discovered there include an elaborately decorated helmet, the remains of a round shield, a mail shirt, and a sword having an elaborate hilt (handle) decorated with gold and red garnets, found in a wooden scabbard lined with wool, the oil of which protected the blade. The Sutton Hoo sword was fabricated using a technique known as pattern-welding. First the smith made the blade by twisting rods of steeled iron and forging them to create the core (Figure 38). Then he added a sharp cutting edge.[16]

In the eighth and ninth centuries, Byzantine horse archers were eclipsed, and Byzantine and Islamic military forces both came to depend largely on light cavalry. But the tenth century has been called "the great age of military science in Byzantium." The heavy cavalry was armed with lances; more lightly armed troops wielded javelins, bows, and slings; and an elite infantry was provided with horses, making it highly mobile. Byzantine military planning was always focused on the defense of Constantinople, which was made easier by the city's peninsular location and massive fortifications.[17]

Simon Coupland's study of Carolingian arms and armor in the ninth century underscored the difficulty of ascertaining how military equipment such swords and helmets were actually used. Documents do not always specify variations, and pictorial evidence can be misleading. As for archaeological finds, these may be treasure troves, but by no means do they exist for all equipment or all times. For example, in Carolingian territories armor disappears from graves in the eighth century—whether because it was used less frequently or because it was no longer buried with the dead is an open question. Coupland's careful examination of three kinds of sources—textual, pictorial, and archaeological—resulted in new information about arms and armor. The equipment of the Frankish foot soldier and cavalryman was quite different. The sword was especially important for cavalrymen, and Carolingian smiths learned how to improve its strength and flexibility, making it a highly prized weapon.[18]

Sometimes military technologies from the east traveled west and got incorporated into the equipage of European fighting men. An example is the stirrup, which came from central Asia. The stirrup has been the focus of a classic historical debate, one that begins with a single item of equestrian equipment but touches on much larger issues concerning the nature of warfare in the Carolingian age. In his much-cited *Medieval Technology and Social Change*, Lynn White Jr. argued that the arrival of the stirrup in the eighth century, and its adoption and promotion by the Carolingian ruler of Francia, Charles Martel (c. 688–741), was a technological event of transcendent significance. The stirrup, White said, allowed the emergence of the heav-

Figure 37. *Crossbow with foot stirrup. From Ralph Payne-Gallwey,* **The Crossbow** *(London: Longmans, Green, 1903), figure 25.*

ily armed knight who could engage in mounted shock combat with a lance couched under his right arm. Because he could brace himself, he could charge into an opponent with the full force of his horse, piercing armor with his lance without being thrown.[19]

White further suggested that the high cost of both the equipment and the horses needed for this type of fighting led to feudalism—the social arrangement whereby vassals swore fealty to their lords, pledging service in battle, in exchange for which the lord provided the vassal (now a knight) with a fief, often comprising land, or a manor (discussed in chapter 3). Income from this fief provided the knight with the resources he needed to maintain a warhorse and equip himself for battle. As evidence for this, White pointed to Charles Martel's confiscation of church lands and his gift of some of those lands to his followers. He concluded that the emergence of the heavily armed knight was made possible by the stirrup, and, in turn, that this development brought about feudalism.[20]

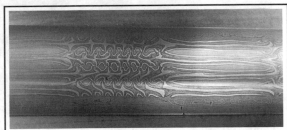

Figure 38. *Section of the blade of a modern replica of the Sutton Hoo sword showing patterning. Replication by Scott Lankton. Photo credit: Steven A. Walton.*

White's brilliant synthesis, which was debated extensively and provoked much new research, ultimately was rejected by military historians, most convincingly by Bernard Bachrach. On the basis of a thorough analysis of the primary sources as well as archaeological data from burial-sites, Bachrach questioned whether stirrups were widely used in the Carolingian age, or even highly valued. He also questioned whether Charles Martel's land policies, which actually resembled those of his predecessors quite closely, should be called feudalism. Later, Bachrach added that the development of mounted shock combat, which he placed in the eleventh and twelfth centuries, depended not just on stirrups, but rather on a combination of elements: a particular kind of saddle with a rigid back-plate (called a cantle), a high pommel, and double girthing or breast collars, all in addition to stirrups. Along with other scholars, Bachrach effectively demolished the notion that the technology of equine equipage brought about feudalism and an equestrian aristocracy. Rather, as Andrew Ayton suggested, an existing military aristocracy "adopted new equipment when it became available, and pursued the tactical possibilities which the equipment offered."[21]

The heavily armed knight became, nevertheless, a significant feature of warfare in the west by the eleventh century (Figure 39). His extensive equipment required the skilled craftwork of the armorer and metalworker. His *hauberk* or mail shirt was made of some 25,000 rings. His sword, lance, and other equipment were equally costly and elaborate. Armorers fabricated various kinds of armor, but the three main types were mail, quilted fabric and leather, and plate armor. Though each type had been known in the ancient world, plate virtually died out by the third century and metal armor made between about 600 and 1250 was almost exclusively mail. After that, various types of plate armor came into use, along with a type of helmet called a *bascinet*.[22] (See Figure 40.)

Figure 39. *Image of mounted knights in battle. Drawing from Herrad of Landsberg,* Hortus deliciarum, *twelfth century (original destroyed). Note the stirrups and saddles with cantles and pommels, "kite" shields, spears, and lances. From* **Das Lustgärtlein der Herrad von Landsberg**, *ed. Maria Heinsius (Kolmar im Elass: Alsatia Verlag, n.d.), plate 10.*

The traditional view of feudal warfare, in which the relationship of lord and vassal is considered central, has been called into question. To paint a picture of Carolingian armies made up of knights and their vassals, bound together by mutual legal and moral obligations, is to oversimplify a much more complex reality. Lords and vassals were part of Carolingian armies, to be sure, but these armies also included significant numbers of foot soldiers, including archers. Timothy Reuter warned of the many gaps in our knowledge about the warfare of this period, suggesting that the ability of leaders to command followers may have had more to do with "charisma, military reputation and ability to award service" than to the mutual legal obligations of feudal relationships. The role of cavalry, especially heavily armed cavalry, has been overestimated.[23]

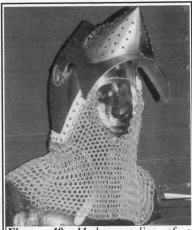

Figure 40. *Modern replica of a bascinet, the most popular head-defense after c. 1220. Replication by Robert Macpherson. Photo credit: Steven A. Walton.*

THE VIKINGS

Scandinavian peoples entered actively on to the stage of western European history from the eighth to the eleventh centuries, as raiders, as conquerors, as new settlers. Though called a variety of names by the peoples who encountered them—Norse, Northmen, Danes, pagans, foreigners, Rus—the appellation Viking was given them by the English and it stuck. Evidence for Viking warfare and military technology is of two kinds: written sources, of which contemporary examples are almost entirely hostile; and artifacts recovered from Viking burials, including human and animal bones, weapons, armor, and ships. The Vikings practiced a polytheistic religion that included a high-status warrior-god named Odin, and a god Thor who controlled elemental forces such as wind and rain. They were a seafaring people who began raiding southward in the ninth century, fighting for booty by attacking settlements or monasteries, and also fighting for control of territory. Often they were aided by alliances with groups in England and Francia who sought support in fighting their own nearby enemies.[24]

Viking weapons are well known because of the thousands of examples found in male burials. Similarly, plundered jewelry and other artifacts have been found in female graves. For Viking warriors, the most important weapon was the sword. It was fabricated with a double-edged blade and was used as a slashing instrument. The best swords were pattern-welded—hammered into shape from a bundle of iron rods and then fitted with steel cutting edges. Blades, made by skilled metalworkers, were imported from the Rhineland. Some particularly fine examples are inscribed with the name Ulfberht, presumably the name of the metalworker who made them, and his successors. The Vikings finished these imported blades in their own workshops. Other weapons included bows and two types of spear: one similar to a javelin, for throwing, and a heavier one for hand-to-hand combat. The Vikings used axes for fighting as well as for cutting timber. They carried round shields made with a core of wood, covered with leather, and furnished with a metal rim, and they wore conically shaped leather helmets with nose-guards (but never with horns, a figment of the modern imagination). In contrast to the popular conception of Vikings as seafarers exclusively, they often used horses for mobility and convenience.[25]

Still, their most significant technologies were the Viking ship and their navigational techniques. Most Scandinavian settlements were close to the sea. Because political power depended on control of the sea, ships were endowed with great symbolic import. There were many different types, but most ships were slim, lightly built vessels that were rowed. The earliest Scandinavian sailing ship yet discovered dates from about 820, and was found Oseberg, west of Oslo (Figure 41). Ships that are only a century newer reveal many changes and improvements.[26]

For shipbuilding, the Scandinavians had access to abundant forests. They felled trees with long-shafted axes, split tree-trunks with wedges, and then trimmed

Figure 41. *The Oseberg Ship, c. 850, Viking Ship Museum, Bygdoy, Norway. Photo credit: Werner Forman/Art Resource, New York.*

planks with short-shafted broadaxes. They built the hulls by the so-called clinker method: first a shell, then overlapping strakes or planks with joints made watertight by means of resin-soaked wool yarn. (See Figure 47 on page 81.) The "long ship" was the conveyance that the Vikings used for their oceanic forays to the south, sometimes with horses aboard. Such a vessel, discovered in Gokstad in southern Norway, had sixteen pairs of oars and would have carried a crew of about thirty-five. It also possessed a mast and sail. Particularly in battles with each other, the Vikings used their ships as mobile fighting platforms. A more significant use, however, was for transporting fighting men to far-away places, for plunder or for establishing a base camp; in their raids the Vikings usually disembarked and attacked on land.[27]

SIEGE WARFARE

The proliferation of castles and their transition from wood to stone—along with the augmentation of urban fortifications in both the east and west—led to the increased importance of siege warfare, especially in the twelfth century (Figure 42). Although castles and walled towns generally had a defensive purpose, they could also operate offensively by serving as operational bases for mobile forces, supply centers, and garrisons. As stone castles proliferated, new siege weapons were developed to attack them. With wooden castles, offensive tactics had included tunneling under walls and setting them afire. When stone construction rendered fire less effective as an offensive weapon, mobile siege towers and battering rams became more important, and especially artillery machines.[28]

Figure 42. *Knights holding kite shields attacking a castle. The mail armor includes a mail shirt or hauberk; weapons include torches, spears, axes, and swords. Drawing from Herrad of Landsberg,* Hortus deliciarum, *twelfth century (original destroyed). From* **Das Lustgärtlein der Herrad von Landsberg,** *ed. Maria Heinsius (Kolmar im Elass: Alsatia Verlag, n.d.), plate 9.*

Such machines are the subject of long-standing controversy. The most important siege weapons of the ancient Greeks and Romans derived their energy from the release of twisted animal sinew or tendons—*torsion* artillery, generally called catapults. Whether the use of such devices ended in late antiquity or continued on into the medieval era is a question that is complicated by an ambiguous terminology. Nevertheless, it is clear that another type of artillery based upon the rotation of a lever, which was invented in ancient China, had become a regular feature of medieval siege warfare by the eleventh century. The generic term for such artillery was trebuchet, but it came in many variations.[29]

Paul Chevedden described the various sorts of trebuchets that developed after the sixth century and replaced the stone-throwing machines of antiquity, a complex collective development that spanned China, Byzantium, Islam, and western Europe. The basic trebuchet consisted of a beam that pivoted off-center on an axle; there was a short arm and a long arm, on which a sling for throwing a projectile was placed. With a traction trebuchet, a gang of strong men suddenly pulled ropes attached to the short arm, and thereby jerked the long arm upward, throwing the missile from the sling. Hybrid forms of the trebuchet utilized both ropes and counterweights, but the most important variant, which derived its power from a counterweight alone, appeared in the twelfth century (Figure 43). Using a counterweight permitted a longer sling and thereby increased the range; such a machine could throw a 33-pound stone 200 yards.[30]

Chevedden noted that the counterweight trebuchet "represents the first significant mechanical utilization of gravitational energy." It was more powerful than previous siege weapons. In addition, by changing the size of the counterweight and the pivotal length, the range could be varied, thereby making it far more accurate. In revising previous assumptions of an Arab origin, Chevedden argued for a Byzantine invention by the engineers of Alexius I Commenus (1048–1118) as an aid to Latin knights in the siege of Nicea during the First Crusade (1096–99). As the trebuchet spread westward, it shifted the balance of power

Figure 43. *A counterweight trebuchet, with weight box at upper right. At far left is a winch with a rope wrapped around it, used to pull up the weight box. The trebuchet has a long sling that rests on a beam; the pouch of the sling holds the shot. When the machine is fired, the weight box loaded with stones falls to the ground, the beam swings up, and the sling pulls the shot up and flings it with great force. From Conrad Kyeser,* Bellifortis, c. 1405, Cod. Phil. 63. *Courtesy Niedersächsische Staats-und Universitätsbibliothek, Göttingen.*

from besieged to besieger; in response, castle design was modified with higher walls and towers. The trebuchet was superseded only by the gradual development of gunpowder artillery beginning in the fourteenth century.[31]

NAVAL WARFARE

Like maritime commerce, naval warfare in the medieval era took place in two primary arenas—the North Atlantic Ocean and the Mediterranean Sea. The Mediterranean has no tides, is usually calm, and has predictable currents and winds. The Atlantic, in contrast, is a vast, powerful, and ever-changing ocean that encompasses a wide range of climates. These environmental factors had significant implications for medieval naval warfare. For the Mediterranean, John Pryor has analyzed physical geography and meteorological conditions along with the technology of medieval ships. He argued that the combination of physical geography and ship technology "had a profound effect on the course of conflict and competition between Islam and Christendom over a very long period of time." The west and Byzantium enjoyed a great advantage over the Muslims because the northern Mediterranean, which they controlled, was more readily navigable and posessed many more naturalized ports than the southern part of the sea contiguous to Islamic lands in northern Africa.[32]

At the end of the sixth century, the Byzantine Empire controlled the entire Mediterranean, challenged only occasionally by Sasanian and eventually by Islamic ships. The Arabs developed a Mediterranean naval force during the next century, after the Byzantines had attempted to recapture Egypt in a naval attack. Arab knowledge of navigation had been gained through centuries of seafaring in the coastal areas of the Red Sea and the Persian Gulf. The first Islamic fleet was built in Egypt, and all qualified sailors (most of whom were Christian) were required to register. Persian and Iraqi shipwrights were brought to new Islamic ports on the eastern Mediterranean. The Islamic warship was a galley with 140 to 180 oarsmen, who were arrayed in two banks, and with as many as three masts. Called a *shini*, it was very similar to the Byzantine galley.[33]

In the medieval centuries, specialized warships were uncommon. Merchant ships were used for the transport of troops and supplies, and could also be adapted to combat when necessary. Warships initially were powered by oarsmen, who could provide the necessary maneuverability, but gradually sails replaced oars, especially in the Atlantic. Framed construction, which was gradually adopted by shipwrights, allowed rudders to be fixed to sternposts, a great improvement over previous methods of steering. Sailing ships could be built with higher decks than ships powered by oars, a great tactical advantage in conflicts with oared ships. They also had the advantage of needing much smaller crews.[34]

In sea battles, sailors hurled stones and other missiles at close quarters—even chunks of lime, in an effort to blind their adversaries—and then rammed the enemy ship or grappled in preparation for boarding. A particularly effective Byzantine weapon was Greek Fire, an incendiary material that was projected from a siphon with a bronze tube and could not be extinguished by water. The recipe was held closely secret by Byzantine emperors. Introduced during the siege of Constantinople (673–78), it was reportedly decisive in driving away the Muslim fleet. The goal of most medieval naval battles was not to sink or burn a ship, which was a highly valuable commodity, but to capture it. The line between piracy and warfare was not sharply drawn. Pirates wanted to capture the goods being transported in merchant vessels. Most medieval sea-powers practiced or encouraged piracy at one time or another, even as they were also victimized by it.[35]

The Byzantine Empire and the Islamic states controlled the Mediterranean Sea for several centuries. Byzantine control of northern sea-lanes facilitated the development of Venetian and Genoese trade routes to the eastern Mediterranean. On both land and sea, the eleventh century was an era of Latin expansion. The Normans took southern Italy from Muslim rulers and then pushed them out of Sicily. In 1085, on the Iberian Peninsula, Alfonso VI of Léon-Castile captured Toledo, a city that had been governed by Islamic rulers since the eighth century. These conquests took on a religious flavor, framed as they were as victories of Christianity over the infidel. They constituted significant background for the Crusades—military expeditions by western knights in the eastern Mediterranean and in other lands as well.[36]

THE CRUSADES

The First Crusade (1096–1102) was undertaken in the aftermath of a passionate sermon delivered by Pope Urban II in 1095, in a field near Clermont in France. The Pope exhorted Frankish knights to march east to free Christians from Islamic rule and to free the Holy Sepulchre in Jerusalem. Thus began a long series of campaigns that continued through the fifteenth century. The First Crusade resulted in the capture of Jerusalem and the establishment of a Latin presence in the eastern Mediterranean. John France noted that important determinants of this victory included the religious zeal of the attackers and the inability of the defenders to understand their "all or nothing mentality." Other factors favoring victory included aid by the Byzantine state and internal divisions within the Islamic states. The complex history of warfare between western and Islamic powers during the next two centuries was marked by victories and defeats on both sides.[37]

The Crusades led to the creation of military religious orders such as the Templars, founded in Jerusalem in 1120, and to the transformation of existing religious orders into military orders, such as the Hospitalers of St. John. In such orders, brothers served as knights and sergeants-at-arms. Knights wore more elaborate armor than sergeants and brought three or four horses, while sergeants had only one mount and might be used as infantry. The military orders built numerous castles in the eastern Mediterranean and also gained control of castles already in place. Often Christian nobles donated their castles to the military orders when they themselves could no longer adequately defend them. The military orders were assisted by other crusaders, by their vassals, and increasingly by mercenaries. In the twelfth and thirteenth centuries, they pursued their own policies throughout Palestine and Syria. Although they usually fought on land, by the end of the 1300 the Templars and the Hospitalers both possessed sizable fleets.[38]

The Crusades involved complicated problems of organization, transport, and supply for a large numbers of fighting men and their horses. By the time of the Third Crusade in the 1190s, crusaders were arranging to head east in ships from several Mediterranean ports, particularly Venice, Pisa, Genoa, and Marseilles. This had been made feasible by the development of large ships that could transport horses, without which the crusading knights were completely ineffective. Ships also transported food and weapons. While equipment could be purchased on arrival, the sudden demand created by hundreds of crusaders would naturally mean high prices.[39]

Western successes were not solely the result of superior weapons and equipment. Knights were able to fight successfully in the eastern Mediterranean because of the power struggles within Islamic territories. In the eleventh century, a group of Turkish peoples originally from Asia, the Seljuks, controlled a large empire, including Syria, with only nominal oversight by the Abbasid Caliphs in Baghdad. The long struggle of the Seljuks with the Fatimid Caliphs of Egypt was indicative of an Islamic world that was far from unified. As Islamic hegemony waned, among the divisions that opened up was that between the Sunni (followers of the *sunni*, the words and deeds of the prophet and his companions) and the Shi'a, who believed that the high authority was held by Muhammad's son-in-law, Ali, and by the imams who were his sons' successors. To complicate matters further, various groups of Christians lived in Islamic lands, some finding preferment and opportunity under Islamic rulers.[40]

In the late eleventh century, the Seljuk Empire was breaking into warring factions. An Islamic army led by Turks and Kurds conquered Egypt in 1169. One of its Kurdish officers, Saladin (1137–93), became the vizier of Egypt and in 1187 won a major battle at Hattin, whereby he gained control of Jerusalem and nearly all of Palestine. Elite Turkish troops led by Saladin used a "composite, recurved bow made of layers of sinew and horn," which, as with the English longbow, could only be handled properly by men who had trained for years. While the ordinary Turkish soldier carried a less powerful bow, and a light lance, sword, or

74

javelin, the Turkish longbow—unlike the English longbow—was a very effective cavalry weapon.[41]

Saladin's great victory over the Levant was what precipitated the Third Crusade of 1189–92. Even though the Crusades were purportedly in support of the Byzantines, during the Fourth Crusade of 1202–04 knights were diverted to Constantinople and captured it, along with much of Greece. Another group from Asia, the Mongols, moved into Islamic regions in the early 1220s, occupied most of Anatolia by the 1240s, and began a program of conquest in the 1250s, occupying Baghdad and Syria by 1260. In Egypt, Mamluk slave soldiers had been employed as shock troops by the Seljuks. But eventually the Mamluks gained control of the country themselves and established the Mamluk sultanate of Egypt and Syria, which lasted until 1517. Struggles between the Mamluks and the Mongols were eventually eclipsed by the expansionism of another group of Turks, the Ottomans, and it was the Ottoman conquest of Constantinople in 1453 that signaled the end of the Byzantine Empire.[42]

* * *

Two primary observations can be made about military technology in the medieval world. The first concerns the general openness and fluidity, and the resulting transmission of military technologies across both cultural boundaries and battle lines. Greek Fire was acquired by the Arabs after the secret was lost by the Byzantines. Beyond Greek Fire, however, there is little evidence for much concern about military secrecy as it pertained to technology. Rather than constituting a barrier to technical transmission, warfare functioned as a stimulant and conduit. Secondly, even though technology was fundamentally important to warfare, most of the decisive victories on the medieval battlefield were determined as much by leadership, political and religious cohesiveness, effective organization, and the relative preparedness of the adversaries. Military technology was never adopted or utilized in a social or political vacuum, and it was never the only component of victory or defeat.

5

TRANSPORTATION, TRAVEL, AND COMMERCE

Transportation entails two essential components—conveyances and infrastructure. During the medieval centuries, land conveyances included wheeled carts and wagons, along with beasts of burden, donkeys, mules, horses, and camels, each with its array of harnesses, hitches, and saddles. Waterborne conveyances, ships and boats, were powered by means of oars, or sails, or a combination of the two. (The term boat is taken to mean a small ship with a specialized purpose, as with a fishing boat, or else a vessel carried aboard a larger vessel, as with a lifeboat.) Infrastructure included roads and bridges, ports, and, in the desert, caravansaries (structures built near oases or towns for accommodating caravans overnight). As in all times, medieval peoples undertook journeys for a great variety of reasons—trade, warfare, diplomacy, adventure, family matters. The importance of pilgrimage as a religious practice among Christians and Muslims prompted many ordinary people to travel long distances to Mecca and Rome and to other holy places.[1]

ROADS, WHEELED VEHICLES, AND BEASTS OF BURDEN

Within the vast area that had been the ancient Roman Empire, Roman roads continued in use throughout the medieval period. Even though these had been extremely well constructed, typically of stone, as time passed many fell into disrepair. Moreover, medieval patterns of trade were not served particularly well by the Roman road system, which had been built primarily for the rapid movement of armies. Some Roman roads were kept up—particularly in the Byzantine Empire—some were abandoned as they deteriorated, others were dismantled so building stones could be used elsewhere. In his study of English medieval roads, Paul Hindle distinguishes several uses evident in road names: salt roads, corpse roads (used to carry corpses to authorized burial sites), pilgrimage roads, and drove roads, on which herds of animals were driven. In general, medieval roads in the west were poorly built and poorly maintained. Often they were barely passable in the winter. Highway robbery was also commonplace.[2]

In the early medieval west, oxen were the most common beasts of burden. Later, horses and mules came into increasing use, following the development of a more efficient horse collar, or, in southern Europe, the breast strap harness. Oxen were relegated to difficult terrain. The transition from oxen to horses occurred during the twelfth and thirteenth centuries, in concert with the expansion of urbanism and long-distance trade. During the entire medieval era, trains of pack animals—donkeys, horses, mules, camels—were a common mode of transporting goods.[3]

In late Roman times, goods were transported in light horse-drawn carts with spoked wheels and extendable sides for increasing capacity. Heavy oak carts pulled by oxen were also common. Both types were two-wheeled. Four-wheeled wagons were generally avoided because they lacked a pivoting front axle that would give them a reasonable turning radius, although aristocrats used four-wheeled coaches. In addition to wheeled vehicles, sledges mounted on runners were used in many situations, including rough terrain and, of course, snow.[4]

As long-distance trade developed, the upkeep of roads gradually improved. Such maintenance was the responsibility of individual landholders, towns, and villages. Drainage was facilitated by means of roadside ditches, the traversing of wetlands by the construction of raised roads called causeways, often with logs for paving. Roads were occasionally paved with stone rubble from quarries, particularly those leading into towns. The construction of stone cathedrals and castles during the eleventh century necessitated the construction of roads capable of sustaining heavy loads, but medieval roads never had the elaborate foundations characteristic of Roman roads; stones were laid directly on the ground. Nobles and princes eventually took it upon themselves to rid their roads of brigandage, a storied hazard of travel, and to refrain from that activity themselves.[5]

The donkey or ass, small and docile, was widely used throughout Europe and the Mediterranean both as a pack animal and for riding (Figure 25). The versatile mule, a cross between a horse and a donkey, was used for individual travel, as a pack animal, and for pulling wagons and canal boats. The most common draft animal was the ox. An improved saddle and the introduction of the stirrup and iron horseshoe made horseback riding increasingly attractive to a wider range of travelers, including those with limited equestrian skill. In Ireland, Celtic chiefs rode in horse-drawn chariots.[6]

Building roadways often involved the construction of bridges, which were usually wooden in the early medieval west. During the eleventh century, stone bridges became more common, along with stone castles and cathedrals. Even stone bridges required a substantial amount of timber, for scaffolding and for the centering needed to build arches. In her study of medieval French bridges, Marjorie Nice Boyer notes the introduction of many innovations: "novel shapes for arches and cutwaters [wedge-shaped piers that divide the current and are less susceptible to damage by floating ice], an improvised method of founding piers, and the use of a sand-lime mortar and of small stones. . . ." Bridges often combined stone arches and timber roadways. Piers were sometimes erected on "starlings," piles driven into the riverbed side-by-side to create an enclosure that reached above the waterline and was then filled with rubble, thereby forming an island.[7]

Donald Hill has described a type of bridge common in Iraq, the pontoon bridge, a plank roadway anchored to boats that were strung across a river on chains running from one bank to the other. In the tenth century there was a pontoon bridge across the Tigris River at Baghdad. Another type of bridge seen both in Islamic lands and in the west was the arch bridge.[8] (See Figure 44.)

Figure 44. *Twelfth-century arch bridge over the Rio Arga, built under Reina Mayer on the camino to Santiago de Compostela, a major pilgrimage site in Puente la Reina, Spain. Note the cutwaters on the bridge piers. Photo credit: Isabel Silva/Art Resource, New York.*

CAMELS AND CARAVANS

Roads were essential only if travel and transport depended on wheeled vehicles. As Richard Bulliet demonstrated, during the medieval centuries wheeled vehicles completely disappeared from an immense expanse of territory running from Morocco to Afghanistan, including Syria, Palestine, Egypt, and Arabia. In our own time, when good roads denote technological progress, this disappearance of roads and wheeled transport might seem like regression. The reality was quite different, as Bulliet pointed out: "the greater economy of the pack camel marks its replacement of wheeled transport as a technological advance rather than a step backward."[9] The camel became the common mode of transport, both for riding and packing with cargo (Figure 45).

Figure 45. *Voyage of Joseph with his brothers. Byzantine mosaic, S. Marco, Venice, Italy. Note saddle on camel. Photo credit: Scala/Art Resource, New York.*

A caravan is a convoy of pack animals, accompanied by merchants and perhaps by travelers and pilgrims. Caravans were an important mode of transport across north Africa, in the eastern Mediterranean, and in central Asia. The term is derived from the Persian word *karvan*, originally applied to transport in central Asia and the eastern Mediterranean but now used generally. The use of the single-humped camel (the dromedary) and the two-humped (bactrian) camel marked a significant advance in transport, particularly in desert regions. Not only can camels make headway in sand, they have a unique capacity for storing water and food. Camel caravans facilitated Asian trade and opened up new trade routes across the Sahara.[10]

79

To set in motion a caravan was every bit as complicated a venture as putting to sea in a great ship. In the eastern Mediterranean, merchants from distant cities often undertook joint ventures with caravans. Caravan sizes varied from twenty-five animals to a thousand or more. There had to be a place to stop every twenty or twenty-five miles, a town, oasis, or a caravansary—a building constructed specifically for caravans, with walls, a gate, a large central pen for the animals, and storage areas for the cargo and for supplies and provisions. On the second floor there would be lodgings for the travelers. Islamic rulers often built caravansaries near oases and towns in order to encourage trade.[11]

SHIPS AND SHIPWRIGHTS

With respect to the links between maritime technologies and economies, Richard Unger stressed that the ship was both "a way to move goods and people" and "an instrument for solving the economic problem of scarcity." The relationships between the economy and changes in ship design were complex. Technical knowledge circulated easily among shipwrights, whose aim, Unger wrote, was three-fold—"an increase of carrying capacity, speed and security." Unfortunately, these tended to be in conflict with one another. Designs that increased speed, for example, would decrease capacity.[12]

Figure 46. *Craftsmen building The Ark, a detail from the story of Noah and The Flood in the arcades of the atrium. Fourteenth-century Byzantine mosaic. S. Marco, Venice, Italy. The shipwrights are sawing a plank from a tree-trunk with a frame saw. A straight blade spanned a vertical wooden frame to which handles for the sawyers were attached on both the upper and lower ends. Photo credit: Erich Lessing/Art Resource, New York.*

Although shipwrights developed a variety of designs, both in northern regions and in the Mediterranean, many of their tools were similar. There were tools for hardwoods and tools for softwoods. Most important was a frame saw, which two-man teams of sawyers used to transform fallen trees into timbers and planks (Figure 46). Shipwrights also used a variety of axes, adzes (tools with curved blades that were used for shaping rough timbers), augers and drills, hammers and chisels. Clamps were used to hold planks together, and caulking irons for rendering joints water-tight.[13]

In the early medieval period, two basic traditions of shipbuilding prevailed—so-called clinch-

80

built or "clinker" construction in the north and mortise-and-tenon construction in the Mediterranean. The southern tradition was inherited from the Romans. Shipwrights constructed hulls without framing. Rather, they butted the planks up against one another and secured them together at the edges with rectangular wooden stubs called tenons that fitted into recesses called mortises; then, the whole joint would be pinned together with a dowel. This labor-intensive method was gradually rendered obsolete as shipwrights used fewer and fewer tenons, and, by the tenth century, abandoned them altogether. Instead, they first constructed an internal skeleton, to which they simply nailed planks edge-to-edge and caulked the interstices.

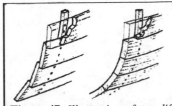

Figure 47. *Illustration of two different kinds of frame construction. On the left is an illustration of clinch built or "clinker" construction with overlapping planks that was practiced in the north. On the right is an example of the type of construction that became common in the Mediterranean by the tenth century. Shipwrights laid the planks edge to edge and nailed them to a frame.*

The strength of the hull now relied not on the skin, as before, but on the skeletal frame. (See Figure 47.) Even though ships built with this method tended to leak more, they were far cheaper fabricate, and they ultimately opened up many new potentialities in ship design.[14]

The Romans had constructed two types of ship, sailing ships and galleys. Galleys derived their primary power from oarsmen, but also had sails. During the tenth and eleventh centuries, the Byzantines built larger and larger war galleys in response to the threat posed by the Islamic naval fleet. All over the Mediterranean, the Roman square sail gave way to the so-called lateen rig, with a triangular sail (Figures 48 and 49). A lateen rig enabled mariners to sail closer into the wind and thereby maneuver more readily. During the tenth century, lateen-rigged vessels gained cargo capacity; as Unger puts it, "the lateen-rigged sailing ship, with a ratio of length to breadth of around three to one, proved to be the workhorse of the Mediterranean commercial revival."[15]

The Arabs were seafarers to the east on the Indian Ocean and beyond from ancient times. By the mid-ninth century they were sailing regularly to China. Our knowledge of these voyagers is derived significantly from Arabic geographical and travel writings from the ninth and tenth centuries, and from archaeological

Figure 48. *View of the harbor of Classe in the time of Theodoric the Great (493–526). Sixth-century Byzantine mosaic. S. Apollinare Nuovo, Ravenna, Italy. Note the vessel with square-rigged sail. Photo credit: Cameraphoto Arte, Venice/Art Resource, New York.*

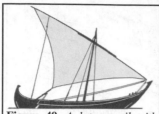

Figure 49. *A lateen sail with characteristic triangular shape.*

finds. Medieval Arab ships of the Indian Ocean had hulls that were "double-ended," coming to a point at both ends, and made of coconut or teak wood, both imported from India. Shipwrights built the hulls with planks placed edge-to-edge that were stitched (rather than nailed) with fiber made from the husks of coconuts. They bored holes along the edges of the planks and then threaded them togeher. Stitching was repaired each year before the ships went to sea. Shipwrights made masts of coconut and teak wood, and fabricated the lateen sails out of coconut or palm leaves or from cotton sail cloth. Sailors guided their vessels with side rudders—one on each side—in the form of oars.[16]

In Europe's Baltic regions, a very different type of ship building called clinker construction (also "clinch built" or "lapstrake") prevailed. With planks overlapping, hulls were more flexible and thus in some ways more durable. Archibald Lewis and Timothy Runyan have cautioned that medieval ships reveal many variations, but, among the basic clinker-built types, most important was the cog, used frequently by a powerful association of German merchants called the Hanse. Cogs had a superstructure called a "castle" aft, sometimes a smaller castle forward, and one large square-sail. Steerage was by means of a rudder attached to the sternpost, and the largest ships reached a capacity of 250 tons. Another type of clinker-built ship was the hulk—tubby, full-ended, flat-bottomed, and fitted with a single mast—which carried commercial traffic on rivers as well as on open waters.[17]

Yet another clinker type was the Viking rowing barge, which was transformed into a ship in the seventh or eighth century by the addition of a square sail and a keel—a timber extending from stem to stern and supporting the entire frame—essential for voyages on open seas. Although all Viking ships were similar, by the ninth century they were becoming specialized in accord with specific function. Lightweight versions carried travelers and cargo on Russian rivers south to Constantinople and the Caspian Sea.[18]

From the eleventh century on, the increase of commercial activity on the Mediterranean, along with the Crusades, led to the construction of larger and larger ships with internal frames. So-called round ships, for transporting bulk cargoes and also passengers, stopped at each port and had to wait for a favorable wind before setting sail again. They were usually lateen-rigged, with two and occasionally three masts. Sailors loaded and unloaded cargo through hatches, and passenger accommodations were in the castles. An Arabic version of this ship was called a *qunbar*.[19]

The nature and extent of trade throughout the medieval world was contingent on complex military, political, and economic factors. Despite ongoing conflicts, there were many commercial contacts among the Byzantines, the Islamic states, and the west. These contacts naturally resulted in cultural and social exchanges, and they facilitated the transmission of knowledge about new technologies.[20]

The Byzantine Empire was a conduit for goods from the east such as silks, spices, and jewelry. Although this eastern trade was disrupted by the Islamic conquests, by the tenth century it was again flourishing. The Byzantines operated a statist system in which they were able to extract numerous tariffs from commercial transactions and to control the flow of goods. It was greatly to the advantage of the Byzantine state that its currency, based on the gold *solidus*, was for centuries preferred for international trade. Eventually, Italian city-states such as Venice, Genoa, and Pisa gained trading privileges in the Byzantine Empire, privileges that proved mutually beneficial at first, but ultimately worked to the advantage of the Italians and to the disadvantage of the Byzantines.[21]

The Islamic conquests opened up a vast expanse of territory wherein trade and travel was relatively free. When the Indian Ocean had been controlled by the Sasanians, trade between Arabia and China was carried out in Sasanian and Chinese ships. But during the ninth century, Islamic powers gained ascendance in the eastern maritime trade. Islamic mercantile communities grew up in India, Ceylon, and along the route to China. Along with the caravan routes through central Asia, the so-called silk road, this seaway facilitated a flourishing trade between east and west. One result was that a whole range of inventions such as paper and gunpowder found their way westward, where they were adopted and transformed in the lands around the Mediterranean. In the tenth and eleventh centuries Egypt became a crossroads for long-distance trade. Muslim and Jewish traders from Maghreb in North Africa and al-Andalus traveled through Egypt on their way to India. Islamic commerce with sub-Saharan Africa also flourished, a trade in which gold and salt were important commodities.[22]

For a time, in the seventh and eighth centuries, the Mediterranean Sea was divided between two rival commercial powers, the Byzantines controlling the north and the Muslims controlling the south. But the division was never absolute, for neutral emporiums were always an ameliorative factor. For example, the island of Cyprus served as neutral ground for the purposes of commercial exchange between Baghdad and Constantinople. Jewish merchants often acted as intermediaries between their Christian and Islamic counterparts. Certain initially small ports became crucial to early medieval Mediterranean commerce. One of these was Amalfi in southern Italy. Another was Venice on the Adriatic Sea. As a result of the rivalry between Byzantine and Islamic powers in the Mediterranean, Venice became an important commercial conduit for the Byzantines, who considered it part of their empire. The Venetian role in east-west trade became especially important after the Islamic conquest of Sicily and parts of southern Italy. Before the year 1000, most sailors plying the Byzantine trade had been Greeks or Syrians. But, gradually, Venice and two other Italian city-states, Genoa and Pisa, became maritime powers in the Mediterranean.[23]

Living as they did on a lagoon, Venetians had to purchase or trade for all their grain. Trading for grain and other necessities, their barges transported goods up the Po and other northern rivers of the Italian peninsula—not only salt and fish, on which they held a local monopoly, but also goods from the east. At Pavia, a commercial crossroads, they sold eastern luxuries to the Lombard and Carolingian kings. Venetians had an advantage in the Pavian market because they were best supplied with luxury goods from the east.[24]

By making various treaties with the lords who controlled the riverways, the Venetians protected their own trade with the north. Because shipwrecks were all-too common, especially important to the Venetians were treaties that excused them from the medieval custom whereby shipwrecks became the property of the ruler in whose territory the wreck occurred. For protection against brigands, Venetian barges traveled in convoys, their crews heavily armed. At many points they were subject to the regulations imposed by local authorities. For example, each barge had a spike called a "key" nailed into the side at the load line, the exact placement being determined by the size of the vessel; the key of an overloaded barge would be under water, and the *nauta* in charge subject to a fine. The *nauta* contracted for cargo and operated the vessel himself. He sometimes carried small-time traders and passengers, but he also transported cargo for wealthy Venetians who were engaged in commercial ventures.[25]

As the Po River Valley became more stable politically and the Italian communes developed, the demand for luxury goods from the east increased, as did the quantity and quality of goods produced by the communes that was available for export, such as woolens. The Venetians were astute participants in this trade, but they also turned to long-distance commerce. They sold slaves captured in the Slavic lands of central Europe to the Byzantines and to the Muslims. Timber was plentiful in nearby forests, and it was in great demand because of the immense quantities required for Mediterranean shipbuilding by both Islamic and Byzantine powers. Despite Papal prohibitions, Venetians sold timber to the Muslims, in return for which they received gold and silver—with which they then bought luxury goods from Constantinople which they sold to the northern Italian city-states. With a ready supply of iron and hemp as well as timber, the Venetians also turned to shipbuilding themselves. In time, they became the leading shippers not only on the Adriatic, but in the eastern Mediterranean as well.[26]

With the aid of new methodologies, Michael McCormick has greatly expanded our knowledge about travel and commerce across the Mediterranean, especially in the Carolingian Age. Because a very large number of medieval primary sources have been digitalized, he was able to search databases for information widely scattered in disparate sources. McCormick has catalogued every mention of travelers in Greek, Latin, and old Slavonic sources between 300 and 900 and has also investigated Arabic and Byzantine sources for the same information. Cataloguing 699 travelers, he has researched their biographies and created an extensive database. He also tracked "things that traveled," such as coins, amber, and relics, as well as slaves. One conclusion of his far-ranging study is that Mediterranean commerce among the Franks, Arabs, and Byzantines was far more extensive between 700 and 900 than had been thought. Further, an important aspect of that trade consisted of the Frankish slave trade.[27]

On the southern shore of the Mediterranean, historians have learned much about shipping, travel, and trade from the Egyptian Geniza documents, especially the hundreds of letters from voyagers to their families, friends, and business partners. These indicate that regular travel between Egypt and the Iberian Peninsula, and between the eastern Mediterranean and Marseilles was nothing unusual. Europeans traders appear frequently in these documents. A commodity commonly sold in Egypt was Brazilwood, grown in the Indies and used to make a red dye. Egyptians also purchased timber and cheese, a staple food of the poorer population. While Egyptian flax and alum, a mordant for dyes, were purchased in large quantities by Europeans, the Egyptian Jews who created the Geniza documents (discussed in Chapter 2) carried out three-fourths of their trade with other Islamic countries.[28]

Business was largely conducted on the basis of friendship and trust, and ties were often strengthened by means of marriages arranged between merchant families in Cairo and those in distant lands—al-Andalus, Tunisia, Morocco, Arabia, Palestine, Lebanon, Syria, Iraq. Hundreds of Geniza documents refer to far-flung travels for the purpose of trading, with little mention of political interference. Jewish traders frequently traveled on Muslim ships. Skilled artisans seem to have been highly mobile throughout Islamic lands. S. D. Goitein characterized the Mediterranean between the eleventh and thirteenth centuries as "a free trade community." Yet, while there may have been little political interference when crossing boundaries, there were always tolls and taxes as well as manifold physical dangers and discomforts.[29]

THE CONNECTIVITY OF MICROREGIONS

In their groundbreaking work about the Mediterranean world, *The Corrupting Sea*, Peregrine Horden and Nicholas Purcell emphasized the significance of small settlements and local activities. They argued that a focus only on the great trade routes by land and sea, a "top-down" approach, devalues the significance of diminutive boats sailing short distances and carrying local products, an activity spanning the ancient and medieval centuries. Focusing only on major trade routes also ignores the ubiquitous donkey trails and footpaths that linked with the main arteries of overland transport, and linked seaports to their hinterland.[30]

The history of the local transportation networks in the Mediterranean region is marked by "diversification and year-by-year adjustment" to shortages or surpluses. Even if the volume of luxury trades waned, the needs of the poor were constant, and this could generate significant interregional trade in food, cloth, and clothing. Interregional demand could be fueled by small changes in the amount of rainfall from one year to the next.[31]

This perspective on the history of the Mediterranean runs counter to a traditional historiography that emphasizes the rise of the Italian cloth industry, specialization and mechanization, industrial capitalism and technological progress. Horden and Purcell insisted that "most clothing production remained local," and

85

that "the great expansion of the trade was a gradual process which began only with specialized production of very high-value fabric." Furthermore, the production of commodities such as cloth was centered neither where raw material was produced nor where finished goods were mostly consumed. The development of the large-scale production of the later medieval period emerged from "universal local and small-scale redistribution systems." Redistribution—that is, taking resources out of one microregion and transferring them to another—depended on the activities of the ubiquitous small trader.[32]

LONG-DISTANCE TRADE

In northern Europe, trade and commerce were promoted by an association of German merchants called the Hansa. The Hansa succeeded because it connected the immense quantities of raw materials from eastern Europe—timber, furs, metallic ores—to markets in the west. During the twelfth and thirteenth centuries, the Hansa obtained trading concessions all across Europe, creating new towns in northern and central regions, controlling commerce in the Baltic region, and ultimately, in the late medieval period, penetrating established European markets. Hansa conveyances included the cog and later the hulk, and, in terms of infrastructure, a great network of roads and pathways. Eventually more than two hundred towns belonged to the Hansa, including Hamburg and Lübeck (the Hansa capital) in the west and Gdansk (Danzig) and Rostock in the east.[33]

The Crusades stimulated production and commercial exchange as thousands of individuals moved from west to east. Angeliki Laiou, who has investigated the role of the Byzantines in supplying the Crusaders, pointed to several significant developments: the connection between the Crusades and the growing involvement of Italian merchants in the eastern Mediterranean; the growing importance of Byzantine merchants and bankers involved in international money transactions; the evolving laws of the sea regarding reparations and reprisals for losses; and, finally, commercial and political communication between Byzantines and Muslims.[34]

* * *

Medieval trade involved long routes and short routes; it involved roads, oceans, and waterways. It continued in peacetime and wartime. Indeed, warfare profoundly affected supply and demand and, therefore, the volume of trade. Commercial exchange also facilitated other kinds of exchange, including the transfer of new inventions and new ideas, and the exchange of texts and, more broadly, of knowledge itself. As the Geniza documents vividly attest, trade entailed communication. Communication and the technologies of writing were crucial modalities, first, in linking individuals within local cultures and ultimately in connecting them to distant cultures both contemporary and historic.

6

COMMUNICATION

Communication is a term that covers many human activities, more in modern times than in the medieval centuries, but a significant range even then—speaking and listening, the creation of pictorial images and observation of those images, writing and reading, communication over distances—was a direct function of transportation. This chapter focuses on technologies of communication, particularly writing and reading. It treats writing implements such as reed pens and quill pens, writing media such as inks and pigments, writing surfaces such as parchment and paper; and the physical form of the book. Intrinsic to communication are social and cultural issues: orality and literacy, the role and status of pictorial representations, and methods of disseminating both images and the written word. The concept and meaning of literacy was of central import in Byzantium, the Islamic states, and the west. So was the religious context of reading and writing.

WRITING MATERIALS

Writing is applicable to surfaces ranging from stone and wood to fine parchment. Most common in antiquity was papyrus, which remained significant in the early medieval era as well. Made from the stalks of an aquatic plant that was plentiful in the Nile River Delta (Figure 50), papyrus grew as tall as fifteen feet above the water and the pithy stalks could be two inches thick. Beginning around 3000 B.C.E., Egyptians used these stalks to make sheets upon which one could write. Workers peeled off the outer layer and sliced the remaining material into thin strips. They put a layer of these strips on a hard surface and covered them with a second layer positioned horizontally. Then, they treated the whole by wetting it, beating or pressing it, and drying it in the sun. The material exuded a resin that acted as glue, fusing the crisscrossed strips into a solid but flexible sheet that they trimmed and polished with a volcanic glass called pumice.[1]

While single sheets could be used for documents, papyrus was often made into rolls. Workers would attach the edge of one sheet to the next sheet with a flour paste, smoothing the joint flat. The size of a roll was usually about twenty sheets. The resin that held the strips together, when dry, acted as a sizing, preventing ink from soaking through. Scribes could correct errors by wiping off wet ink or scraping off dry ink.[2]

The codex, a book made of folded sheets sewn along one edge, began as a form of papyrus book whose portability made it popular with the early Christians. Scholars debate the reasons for its general adoption as the standard form of the book, but are agreed that, besides being portable, it could be concealed in garments (an important consideration with a persecuted religion), and readily opened to a particular place in the text. Although the codex had generally replaced the roll by the fourth century C.E., the roll continued in use for special purposes throughout the early medieval period, albeit a different kind of roll. In antiquity the papyrus was rolled horizontally. In medieval times, parchment or vellum was rolled vertically, a form useful for lengthy records such as the rolls of exchequer (treasury records) in England , prayer rolls, and genealogies.[3]

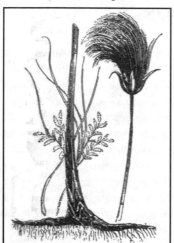

Figure 50. *A drawing of the papyrus plant, from David Diringer,* **The Hand-Produced Book** *(London: Hutchinson's Scientific and Technical Publications, 1953), fig. IV-5, a.*

The term parchment usually refers to sheepskin or goatskin, while vellum refers to calfskin. To produce parchment, leatherworkers soaked skins in a bath of lime for ten days to remove any flesh, and then scraped them. They could make a surface smoother by rubbing it with pumice and could make it whiter by rubbing it with chalk. Parchment and vellum are fine, durable materials, but expensive. A large parchment Bible, for example, required several hundred animal skins.[4]

Paper had its origins in ancient China, where it was made with a variety of bast fibers—the woody fibers obtained from various trees such as the mulberry. By the eighth century, paper was being fabricated in the Islamic regions out of cloth, usually hemp or linen. Papermakers soaked the cloth and hammered it into a pulp which they poured into a rectangular mold framing a cloth sieve. Medieval paper-molds were of two kinds. Sometimes the mold was floated in a vat of water from which the liquid gradually drained out and the sheet was sun-dried while still in the mold. Dipping molds were designed so that the sheets could be removed while still moist; in Europe they were "couched"—pressed between two pieces of wool felt and hung to dry. The mold could be reused while the sheets were drying. Papermaking always entailed sizing—that is, applying glue, gypsum, gum, or starch to make the surface impermeable, so that the paper did not absorb ink like a blotter.[5]

Paper was unknown to the Byzantine and Sasanian empires before the Islamic conquests. As Jonathan Bloom describes it, "the introduction of paper and papermaking across Islamic lands in the ninth and tenth centuries was a remarkable historical and technological achievement that transformed society in its wake." The process of making paper from linen or cotton rags was probably devised in pre-Islamic central Asia (with Chinese bast papers in the background).

88

The key to its rapid spread was the decision of the Abbasid rulers to use paper for their official records. A mill established in Baghdad in 794–95 was capable of turning out sufficient quantities of paper to supersede papyrus and parchment. It showed the potential for producing paper quickly and in large quantities, and far less expensively. Because ink could not be scraped off, as with papyrus or parchment, the information written on a paper document seemed to be trustworthy. Of course non-erasability was also a disadvantage, for paper was too expensive to throw away and could not be used for such transitory purposes as mathematical calculations.[6]

Inks were tailor-made for diverse writing surfaces. Ink prepared from lampblack or carbon bound with plant gum was used on papyrus and paper, but tended to flake off parchment. Lampblack was made by burning various waxes, oils, or resins, and collecting the soot; carbon was made by heating plant products in earthen pots. For parchment, a brown ink was made from gallnuts (swellings on the bark of oak trees caused by insects laying their eggs), which contained gallic acid and tannin. A solution of this substance was mixed with ferrous sulfate. This metal tannate ink penetrated parchment or vellum like a dye, but could not be used on paper because the acids it contained eventually made holes.[7]

Although the Byzantines in Constantinople had extensive contacts with the Abbasid court in Baghdad during the ninth century, they did not adopt paper or the technology of papermaking. Even though these were transmitted from Islamic lands to Christian Europe in the eleventh and twelfth centuries, paper did not become common in Byzantium until the thirteenth. Instead of using paper, Byzantine scribes copied books on parchment codices and legal and state documents on scrolls, first made of papyrus and later of parchment. Once they began using paper, they imported it from Syria and other Islamic lands.[8] One wonders: given their familiarity with paper through Abbasid contacts, why did the Byzantines not adopt paper earlier?

Christians in Europe learned about paper from Islamic Spain and Sicily. By the twelfth century, Europeans were making it themselves, and soon introduced several new techniques, including the use of meshed wire in the molds instead of cloth sieves. To make wire, they cut strips of metal and drew these through successively smaller holes cut into dies made from a harder metal. In Italy, papermaking was taken up in the town of Fabriano on the Adriatic Coast and then in the Veneto. By the end of the thirteenth century, Fabriano paper had begun to dominate Mediterranean markets. The Italians invented watermarks—raised designs on the mold screen—to identify their superior papers. Starch tended to mildew in a climate different from Islamic lands, hence European papermakers made size out of gelatin, produced from the horns, hoofs, and hides of animals. Gelatin sizing made a harder surface that worked better with the quill pens that Europeans had customarily used on parchment. In Islamic lands, writers used reed pens, suitable for writing on the softer paper sized with starch. Further improvements in Italian papermaking involved the mechanization of pulp-making.[9]

Writing and reading are the focus of a large body of scholarship, which in recent times has treated literacy as a historically specific phenomenon, investigating its meanings within particular cultures. This contextual approach has largely superseded an older deterministic tradition which held that literacy changed human mentalities and culture wherever it occurred.[10]

In the modern era, the term literacy assumes knowledge of both reading and writing. In the medieval world, however, far more people could read than could write. Information was often recorded by dictating to professional scribes or secretaries, who were used extensively by ruling elites. Reading entailed speaking aloud, often with the air of a performance, to an extent unfamiliar today. Literacy was not equated with education, rationality, or even intelligence, and in the west the concept was complicated by the distinction between the learned language of Latin and spoken vernaculars; *Litterati* were those who could read Latin, not those who could read their own vernacular languages. Reading and writing were important to governance and administration, and, more broadly, to religious practices. Both Christianity and Islam were centered on a holy book. Because a text could influence the non-literate and semiliterate by being spoken aloud, a high value was placed on rhetoric. As Brian Stock has shown, in eleventh- and twelfth-century Europe, non-literate people were profoundly affected by the use of texts by preachers.[11]

Scholars once assumed high rates of literacy in Greek and Roman antiquity and in the Byzantine world. Recently, however, these assumptions have been reexamined. Margaret Mullet has suggested that Byzantine literacy was low during the seventh and eighth centuries but rose considerably in the ninth and tenth. Book ownership was a privilege of elites because parchment was expensive. Literary production was focused on encyclopedias, summaries, and epitomes. Mullet investigates a different form of writing. The tenth century, she says, was "a golden age of Byzantine letter-writing." Letters facilitated social cohesion; receipt of a letter was accompanied by oral communication from the bearer. The letter was "written, oral, material, visual, and had its own ceremony."[12]

Culture in pre-Islamic Arabia was largely oral, though writing was not unknown. Arabs had highly developed traditions of poetry, a literature created and transmitted orally. The highest poetic form was the ode, called the *qasida* in Arabic. Professional poets composed and then publicly recited poetry, but there was no concept of a particular version that might be "authentic." Rather, an essential aspect of the art of poetry was embellishment and the reworking of traditional material. Muhammad communicated his revelations orally. Although the Koran would play a central role in the spread of reading and writing throughout Islamic lands, recitation from memory remained important to Islamic culture. Great value was placed on memorization of the entire Koran (which is about the same length as the New Testament of the Bible). People honored by the name *hafiz*, meaning one who "knows by heart," could be from any strata of society, they could be female or male, old or young.[13]

Aside from its use in books, letters, and documents, Arabic writing came to be used ubiquitously as ornamentation for the mosque, a phenomenon quite unparalleled in the Byzantine Empire or the west. Because the Koran was considered the actual, literal word or God, copying quotes from it in beautiful writing was considered meritorious. Other pious writings could also be used. Inscriptions might be written anywhere on the exterior or interior of the building and some mosques were covered with inscriptions. They were made with all the materials used for surface decoration and ornamentation, including brick and tiles. Like the Christian icon, an inscription served as "a visible representation of supernatural reality." Many inscriptions on mosques were not immediately readable by the average literate person because they were in highly obscure places or were written in a fashion too intertwined to be readily legible. But any literate person would have memorized much of the Koran, certainly the most familiar phrases that were often used on the walls. Recognition of one word would have brought the entire phrase to mind. And the writing served its purpose as a focus of meditation even if not actually read at all.[14]

In Europe, the number of people able to read declined over time, but there were always some. As monasticism expanded in the seventh century, monasteries became increasingly important as "institutions of religious culture and learning." The education provided by monasteries was supplemented by the development of cathedral schools; a religious school was established at Canterbury, for example, during the first third of the seventh century. Still, literacy was limited to a small number of lay elite and clericals. In the late ninth century, Charlemagne—whose own literacy is problematic—recruited the English cleric Alcuin (c. 730–804) to head his palace school. One of Alcuin's most important achievements was the creation of a small, uniform, easily readable script for writing and copying manuscripts. Known as the Carolingian minuscule, it replaced previous scripts that were virtually undecipherable. Charlemagne's primary goal, aside from educating his own children and grandchildren, was to increase the general level of literacy in his palace and achieve more efficient record-keeping. During

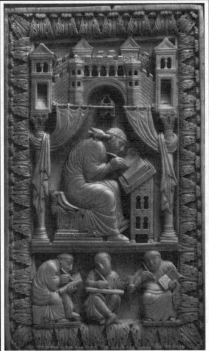

Figure 51. *St. Gregory and three scribes. Ivory, from Metz, Germany, c. 968-980, Kunsthistorisches Museum, Vienna, Austria. Photo credit: Erich Lessing/Art Resource, New York.*

Carolingian times, the availability of books increased markedly due to the development of scriptoria, workshops devoted to the copying of books that were established in Charlemagne's palace and in numerous monasteries. Increased book production was the result of an increase in the number of trained scribes. (See Figure 51.) But despite Charlemagne's reforms, the European west remained primarily an oral culture through the eleventh century.[15]

The consensus among scholars is that western Europe made a transition from an oral to a scribal culture during the twelfth and thirteenth centuries. Contributing factors included the development of large-scale commerce, the growth of towns, and especially the establishment of universities. On the basis of his investigation of English materials from 1066 to 1307, M. T. Clanchy argued that increasing literacy "was indicated by, and was perhaps a consequence of, the production and retention of records on an unprecedented scale." Clearly there was a similar trend in other parts of Europe.[16]

Clanchy describes the acquisition of a "literate mentality" not in broad psychological or philosophical terms, but simply as a "cluster of attitudes which literates in England shared and expressed in all sorts of ways in surviving records." These include the shift from a trust in living memory to a sense that written records needed to be created, and also to the new practice of actually consulting such records from the past. Increasing literacy was not so much a function of broader education as of practical convenience. As Clanchy summarized "in early medieval Europe, the skills of scribes were . . . primarily applied to the arts of worship through the production of liturgical manuscripts . . . . Gradually however despite Christianity being a religion of a book and medieval culture being shaped by monks, writing on parchment was adopted and applied to mundane purposes of government, property owning and commerce."[17]

BOOKS AND ILLUMINATION

In the Byzantine Empire, most books concerned theology and the liturgy. Because of the high cost of parchment and the time it took for a scribe to make copies, books were expensive. The value of one ninth-century manuscript, for example, has been estimated to be the equivalent of half a year's salary for a civil servant. Private collectors rarely owned more than twenty-five books. There was no such thing as a book market. Readers acquired books by commissioning a copy of a manuscript at a scriptorium, or going to a library, or borrowing from friends.[18]

Both in Byzantium and in the west, the decoration of books with small paintings and ornamentation—a process called manuscript illumination—was common in religious books such as psalters and gospels. Usually a scribe would copy an entire book, leaving a space instead of the first letter of the first word of every chapter (Figure 52). Then, a rubricator would add these ornamental rubrics, and illuminators would paint pictures, either in spaces left for them throughout the text or on separate pages. Often the area of a picture would first be gilded, illuminators laying down gold leaf on a binding medium such as gum. Sometimes they would first apply a ground of gesso (a thick, water-base paint made of plaster, gypsum, or chalk and bound with glue), thereby allowing the surface to be tooled after the gold

Figure 52. *Beginning of the Gospel of Saint Luke, England (probably Canterbury), second quarter of the eleventh century. Ms. 709, fol. 78, The Pierpont Morgan Library, New York. Photo credit: The Pierpont Morgan Library/Art Resource, New York.*

leaf was laid down. After gilding, illuminators created pictures by adding pigments—colors derived from plants and various organic substances mixed with a binding medium of glair (clarified egg white) and other substances.[19]

The Byzantines developed miniature painting to a high art. Miniatures were one of four main forms of visual representation in the empire, the others being mosaic, fresco, and icon painting. Through visual images the Byzantines expressed devotion, awe, and other emotions. The paintings might be closely related to the text or they might tell a part of the story not revealed in the text. They also lay at the heart of iconoclasm, a movement aimed at banning religious images in accord with the view that to allow images in holy books or in churches amounted to the veneration of images—prohibited by Christian theology. During two lengthy periods in the eighth and ninth centuries, the imperial policy of iconoclasm resulted in the destruction of thousands of images, many of them in books.[20]

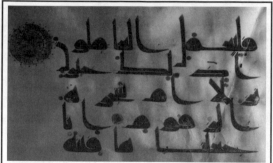

Figure 53. *A leaf from a Koran written in kufic script. Abbasid dynasty (Iraq), ninth century. Collection of Mrs. Bashir Mohamed, London. Photo credit: Werner Forman/Art Resource, New York.*

WRITING AND BOOKS IN ISLAMIC LANDS

Arabic writing developed within a context quite different from that of Byzantium. Pre-Islamic Arab culture had not been profoundly influenced by classical antiquity. The most important literary tradition was that of poetry; writing was reserved for practical matters such as trade and commerce. The pre-Islamic Arabic script took only a cursive form with many of the letters joined by ligatures, and there were many ambiguities. Because this was problematic for the transmission of authentic copies of the Koran, during the seventh century Arabic script was "regularized." Although the revelations of the prophet Muhammad had been transmitted orally at first, soon after his death there began a process of codification. Medieval Islamic writing appeared not only in books, but on cups, vases, textiles, and buildings, and the earliest evidence for a written Koranic text appears on a building, the Dome of the Rock in Jerusalem, completed in 691. But thousands of parchment fragments have also survived. Medieval manuscripts of the Koran were copied on parchment sheets that were put into protective boxes, or else they were sewn and bound into covers made of wood and covered with leather. (See Figure 53.) The importance of the Koran insured that Arabic would become the common language of most Islamic lands. It also encouraged ordinary people to read.[21]

As paper replaced parchment, books "became major vehicles for artistic expression." Calligraphers and illuminators enjoyed high status, their workshops often supported by princes and their courts. Besides the Koran, they created books of poetry and books on astronomy and botany, history and philosophy. Most were intended for sale on the open book market, for which space was reserved in many cities.[22]

An important development in calligraphy occurred when a secretary (a *kuttab* or writer in Arabic) in the Abbasid court of Baghdad invented a new, regularized script that became one of the six that were learned as the standard repertoire of all calligraphers. Along with stylized calligraphies came highly detailed illustrations, especially in technical and scientific works, but not in the Koran. Copies of the Koran could be decorated, but they were never illustrated with images.[23]

Under the Abbasid rulers in the ninth century, secretaries exerted significant influence on the courts. Official documents were judged by their elegance, by their subtle references, and by the skill of the calligraphic hand as well as by their substantive content. Thus did the art of writing move from the primary domain of Koranic copyists to the secular world. The work of writers was facilitated by the use of paper, as well as by a new simplified script called the "broken cursive" and by the use of lampblack ink—all of which contributed to what Jonathan Bloom called "an explosion of books." Under the Abbasids, "books and book knowledge became a general aim of Islamic society." The arrival of paper, the production of books, and the translation of texts from Greek and other languages to Arabic were simultaneous and mutually reinforcing developments. Topics and disciplines addressed in books included theology, law, philology, grammar, biography, history, poetry, philosophy, navigation, practical arts and engineering, astronomy, astrology, mathematics, alchemy, and cooking. There were even works of fiction. Yet, oral transmission was still considered superior to writing, and people would flock to hear scholars read from their writings.[24]

Most Islamic book production was carried out in mosques. An author would sit cross-legged in front of auditor-copyists, as many as a dozen of them, who would take dictation. A close associate or student might sit nearby to serve as an intermediary. Although the author would have written a draft of the work to follow while dictating, he would often speak from memory. A copy of a book was not considered authentic unless "authorized," a process accomplished by "check-reading," with the scribe reading the text back to the author. This enabled an author to create multiple copies from a single reading. The proliferation of books supported many new professions—copyists, bookbinders, dealers in paper, and, of course, book dealers. Numerous libraries, both private and public, were established throughout Arab lands.[25]

WRITING AND BOOKS IN THE WEST

Book production in the early medieval west was carried out for the most part in the monastic scriptorium. A book might be copied by five or more scribes working in shifts or by a single scribe. Later, with the expansion of schooling and the establishment of universities, secular workshops flourished in many towns; sometimes, professional stationers contracted parchmenters, scribes, and illuminators who might specialize in elaborate border decorations or in miniature pictures. The stationers also supervised the *pecia* (piece) system that developed in the thirteenth century. Under this system, pieces of university-approved copies of texts were hired out by stationers to scribes for copying. The system entailed an elaborate system of checking copies against the original for accuracy.[26]

As to the secular scribes who made official records, wrote letters, and copied dictation, their most important tool was a wooden tablet covered with wax and folded into a diptych—that is, two hinged leaves that could be closed like a book. The scribe could make notes on such a tablet and then transfer the writing to parchment. Authors also wrote original drafts on such wax tablets and then had copies made on parchment.[27]

A book was made with "gatherings" of parchment. In both the Byzantine Empire and in the west, a piece of parchment would be folded into a bifolio—two large leaves making four pages—which was then folded again to make a "quire" of four leaves that were half the size, thereby forming eight pages. The size of the book was determined by the way the sheets were folded. In the folio, the sheets are folded once, in the quarto twice, and in the octavo, three times. When books were sold in a market, they were often unbound. Binding was a specialized craft in which the pages of a manuscript were sewn and secured by covers. There were two stages. The first, called forwarding, involved sewing the leaves together and attaching the covers. Medieval covers were made of wooden boards usually covered with leather. The second, finishing, involved decoration of the covers, often by impressing designs into the leather with heated brass tools, a process called tooling. Binding was different in Europe, where text reads from right to left, than in Arabic lands, where text reads in the opposite direction and the spine is on the right rather than the left.[28]

THE TRANSMISSION OF KNOWLEDGE

Throughout the medieval centuries, books—as with technical skill, information, and expertise of various kinds—were exchanged across the borders of Byzantium, the Islamic states, and the west. Sometimes, this communication took place after territory was occupied by a victorious power, as happened all across North Africa and on the Iberian Peninsula after the Islamic conquests. There were numerous other occasions for such exchange in the course of commercial dealings. Travelers and pilgrims would acquire knowledge of foreign cultures and impart this knowledge to those back home. Also, formal diplomatic missions became commonplace in the later medieval centuries.

In addition to formal and informal exchanges, there were two great periods of translation during the medieval centuries. The first was centered in Baghdad in the eighth and early ninth centuries, when the entire corpus of Greek mathematical, scientific, and technical learning was acquired by the Abbasids. The Abbasid court and governmental administration developed a secular bureaucracy and encouraged learning of all kinds. Among the ranks of courtiers and administrators, there were not only Arabs but also Syrians, Persians, and people from other cultures, some more learned and sophisticated than their Arab rulers. Perhaps this was a factor in the far-reaching search for books that began under Harun al-Rashid (786–809), who sent agents to Byzantium in quest of manuscripts. Harun's son, al-Mamun (813–33), created the House of Wisdom as part of the Abbasid court. From these beginnings, the corpus of Greek medicine; Greek philosophy, including the works of Plato and Aristotle; Greek mathematics, including Euclid's *Elements* and Ptolemy's *Almagest*; and the writings of the Hellenistic engineers Philo and Hero of Alexandria were translated into Arabic and became the basis for extensive Arabic commentaries and original works of Islamic learning.[29]

A second period, "the great age of translation," occurred in the west, primarily in the twelfth and thirteenth centuries. This had been preceded by western victories over Islamic forces in Spain and in Sicily, which put western powers in control of centers of Arabic learning. An increased interest in learning in the west, along with curiosity about antiquity, meant that scholars would come from all over Europe to aid bilingual and trilingual Spanish scholars, Jewish, Islamic, and Christian, in the translation of books from Arabic into Latin. Thus was the west to acquire a knowledge of antiquity and of the Arab world, knowledge that would serve as a foundation for the new universities.[30]

* * *

Intellectual life and the world of learning are often treated separately from the techniques writing and making books. Yet the crafts of book-making and book decoration, of writing and copying, were intrinsic to the creation of a book's contents. Moreover, the communication that lay at the heart of writing, disseminating, and reading books was informed by broader cultural and political movements, most importantly religious movements, but also by political and cultural power, and by patronage. These in turn were influenced by trade and travel, and by warfare. While the medieval book was a craft object, the history of that book encompassed a much broader history including diverse traditions of interchange and communication among contiguous societies and cultures.

CONCLUSION

The material world and the technologies that humans use to manipulate and shape that world are profoundly embedded in historical cultures such as those described in this booklet. Aside from specialists in archaeology and the history of technology, this reality has often escaped the attention of scholars, teachers, and students. Nevertheless, the embeddedness of material culture and technology in daily life is true for all people, whether men, women, or children, whether wealthy and powerful or poor and powerless, whether living in a castle, a palace, a hut, or a tent. The expression *daily life* bears emphasis. This booklet has suggested that an exclusive focus on grand overarching themes such as "progress," or on problematic phenomena such as "invention," obscures the degree to which everyday technologies are woven into the warp and weft of human affairs.

Scholars and students of medieval technology, especially early medieval technology, must confront a problem, namely a scarcity of sources, and must face the realization that much of what happened in the medieval centuries will remain elusive. At the same time, new investigative techniques and new approaches to the history of technology will continue to provide new information and new analytical insights. An example is the emerging discipline of underwater archaeology. The excavation of sunken ships reveals much about shipbuilding and seafaring, but tells us as much or more about everyday objects, about weapons, about all sorts of past technologies. Another example involves the reexamination of familiar artifacts with new questions in mind; historical tools and implements in museum collections come to mind, as do *amphorae*, the ubiquitous earthen vessels of past epochs with two handles and a narrow neck, which can now be dated more accurately than was once the case. Other new approaches include the use of computer technologies to search primary documents and DNA studies of medieval remains.[1] And of course the reexamination of textual sources with new questions in mind remains at the core of research in the history of technology, as in all history.

While some questions can never be fully answered because the sources will not permit, others are not presently answered because they have not been asked. A case in point pertains to the relationship of gender and technology in the medieval era, a particularly significant relationship because technological activities were frequently assigned and divided according to gender. How exactly were they divided? What did women do and what did men do? How did gender matter in specific historical cultures? These are the sort of questions that must be investigated without projecting modern sensibilities onto past historical epochs. While some of our questions remain unanswered because evidence is simply not there, much of our ignorance is a direct result of the traditional historiography of technology being cast in "gender-free" terms—that is, anchored in the misapprehension that technology is male. To understand the ubiquity of this misapprehension, one needs only consult the work of one of the authors in this booklet series, Francesca Bray, whose critique of the history of technology as a discipline has served as a wake-up call, at least for some of its practitioners.[2]

Men's and women's work sometimes overlapped. When it was separate, what women did was every bit as "technological" as what men did: the preparation of food and drink, tending fields, fabricating textiles. At the present time, historians of medieval history and technology produce at least a hundred books on warfare and military technology to every one book on textiles. This says much about the state of the discipline, but nothing about the relative importance of warfare and textiles in medieval society. At the basic level of "how things work," looms are every bit as complex technologically as trebuchets, and in many ways far more interesting. Further, "low" technologies involving pots, pans, and cooking implements are wide-open fields, begging for sound historical analysis in widely diverse timeframes and localities.

* * *

Something should be said about this effort to address the medieval Byzantine Empire, the Islamic states, and the west in a single coherent analysis. Historical specializations are grounded in the reading and interpretation of primary sources written in whatever language they may appear and in whatever hand. Often, years of study are required before attempting even elementary investigations. Archaeology requires its own years of specialization. Yet, specialization also leads to isolation. For example, even though there was extensive interchange between the Christian west and Islamic lands at certain times, European medieval history is typically studied with little or no attention to Islamic culture except insofar as the Christian west had to contend with Islam as a military threat. Surely this distorts our understanding of medieval history. Yes, the Islamic lands, Byzantium, and the west each had their own history, but it was rarely if ever an isolated history. Addressing all three together—all three in context, as it were—enables us to understand and interpret historical interactions that are not otherwise evident.

Treating the three entities in isolation has had a particularly distorting effect on studies in the history of technology, much the same effect as treating "invention" in isolation, or, rather privileging invention. It is true that source materials elucidating the social and cultural context of medieval invention are quite often scarce. But that is no reason to portray inventions and technological systems merely as inert objects that were punted from Asia to Islam to the west, where, having reached a "progressive" culture, they then underwent significant improvement. Or, from another point of view, no reason to focus on claims that

100

one or another invention appeared in Islamic lands first of all, before anywhere else. In any such scenario, technology's social and cultural context is mostly forgotten, as is the perception that societies might adopt and use technologies appropriate to their own peculiar cultural needs, rather than the progressivist conceits of others.

Even with investigations of specific technologies, cross-cultural comparisons and interdisciplinary perspectives can yield important new insights. An example of how this can work is Finnbarr Barry Flood's study of the monumental water clocks in the Great Mosque of Damascus. One of these clocks was probably built in the eighth century when the mosque was founded, the second in the twelfth century. This second clock had twelve doors out of which birds popped every hour, a set of rotating discs that signaled cosmological events such as the sunrise in the signs of the zodiac, and other features similar to those of clocks described by al-Jazari in 1206. Flood considered this clock in the context of Umayyad political and religious culture. He alluded to its origins in the tradition of Byzantine clocks in Syria and described the wide dissemination of such clocks in the Arab world. He called attention to clocks bestowed as gifts by the Arabs on western rulers such as Charlemagne, and to their diffusion in western regions such as al-Andalus. Even though Flood was primarily concerned with the clock of Damascus and its relationship to the power of the caliphs there, his allusions to a rich context suggest a topic that could be developed significantly in a cross-cultural context.[3] Ideally, such a study would focus both on technology and on social and cultural uses and meanings of technology. One can think of numerous other topics, from trebuchets to textiles, that might be investigated more informatively within a similar cross-cultural methodology.

The aim of this booklet has been to demonstrate the value of thinking about technology and technological systems as they were embedded within specific medieval societies, but as also transferable to other medieval cultures. Thinking about technology across traditional boundaries in this way facilitates a comparative perspective. It also facilitates a method of investigating intensely localized technological phenomena without losing sight of the connections that localities may have had with separate but contiguous societies, political entities, and cultural and economic systems that spanned whole continents.

NOTES

INTRODUCTION

1. Peregrine Horden and Nicholas Purcell, *The Corrupting Sea: A Study of Mediterranean History* (Oxford: Blackwell Publishers, 2000).

2. For the Byzantine Empire, see Warren Treadgold, *A History of the Byzantine State and Society* (Stanford, Calif.: Stanford University Press, 1997); for an introduction, see Robert Browning, *The Byzantine Empire*, rev. ed. (Washington, D.C.: Catholic University Press, 1992). For Islamic lands, see Ira M. Lapidus, *A History of Islamic Societies*, 2d ed. (Cambridge: Cambridge University Press, 2002); for the west, see Robert Bartlett, *The Making of Europe: Conquest, Colonization and Cultural Change, 950–1350* (London: Allen Lane, Penguin, 1993).

3. Economic historians who take a different view of technological progress include Joel Mokyr, *The Lever of Riches: Technological Creativity and Economic Progress* (New York: Oxford University Press, 1990) and David Landes, *The Wealth and Poverty of Nations: Why Some Are So Rich and Some So Poor* (New York: W. W. Norton, 1998).

4. For the Byzantine Empire, see Browning, *Byzantine Empire*; Cyril A. Mango, *Byzantium: The Empire of New Rome* (New York: Charles Scribner's Sons, 1980); Treadgold, *History of the Byzantine State*. For recent research, see Mango, ed., *The Oxford History of Byzantium* (Oxford: Oxford University Press, 2002).

5. See esp. Heinrich Fichtenau, *The Carolingian Empire*, trans. Peter Munz (Toronto: University of Toronto Press and the Medieval Academy of America, 1978); Rosamond McKitterick, ed., *The New Cambridge Medieval History*, vol. 2, *c. 700–c. 900* (Cambridge: Cambridge University Press, 1995).

6. Geoffrey Barraclough, *The Crucible of Europe: The Ninth and Tenth Centuries in European History* (London: Thames and Hudson, 1976); Bartlett, *Making of Europe*; Timothy Reuter, ed., *The New Cambridge Medieval History*, vol. 3, *c. 900–c. 1024* (Cambridge: Cambridge University Press, 1999).

7. See esp. Lapidus, *History of Islamic Societies*, 18–44 and Fred M. Donner, *The Early Islamic Conquests* (Princeton, N.J.: Princeton University Press, 1981).

8. Lapidus, *History of Islamic Societies*, 3–196; Donner, *Early Islamic Conquests*.

9. See Richard Hodges and David Whitehouse, *Mohammed, Charlemagne and the Origins of Europe: Archaeology and the Pirenne Thesis* (Ithaca, N.Y.: Cornell University Press, 1983), 1–19, esp. 1–3, the work on which this paragraph is based. For a masterful essay on the context and development of the Pirenne thesis, see Paolo Delogu, "Reading Pirenne Again," in *The Sixth Century: Production, Distribution and Demand*, ed. Richard Hodges and William Bowden (Leiden: Brill, 1998).

10. Hodges and Whitehouse, *Mohammed, Charlemagne*, 4–5; Richard Hodges, "Henri Pirenne and the Question of Demand in the Sixth Century," in *Sixth Century*, ed. Hodges and Bowden, 2–14.

11. Hodges and Whitehouse, *Mohammed, Charlemagne*, 6–9. See also Chris Wickham, "Overview: Production, Distribution and Demand," in *Sixth Century*, ed. Hodges and Bowden, 279–92.

12. Michael McCormick, *Origins of the European Economy: Communications and Commerce, A.D. 300–900* (Cambridge: Cambridge University Press, 2001); McCormick, "New Light on the 'Dark Ages': How the Slave Trade Fuelled the Carolingian Economy," *Past and Present* 177 (November 2002): 17–54; Hodges and Whitehouse, *Mohammed, Charlemagne*, 6–9; Kevin Greene, *The Archaeology of the Roman Economy* (Berkeley and Los Angeles: University of California Press, 1990); Klavs Randsborg, *The First Millennium A.D. in Europe and the Mediterranean: An Archaeological Essay* (Cambridge: Cambridge University Press, 1991). See also Wickham, "Overview," 279–92.

13. Carole Fink, *Marc Bloch: A Life in History* (Cambridge: Cambridge University Press, 1989), 104–65, citation on 149; Lucien Febvre, "Réflexions sur l'histoire des techniques," *Annales d'histoire économique et histoire* 7 (1935): 531–35; Marc Bloch, "Avènement et conquêtes du Moulin à eau," *Annales d'histoire économique et histoire* 7 (1935): 538–63, translated as "The Advent and Triumph of the Watermill," in *Land and Work in Mediaeval Europe: Selected Papers by Marc Bloch*, trans. J. E. Anderson (New York: Harper Torchbooks, 1969), 136–68.

14. Lynn White Jr., *Medieval Technology and Social Change* (Oxford: Oxford University Press, 1962) and *Medieval Religion and Technology* (Berkeley and Los Angeles: University of California Press, 1978). On White as a historian, see Thomas F. Glick, "Lynn White Jr.," in *Encyclopedia of Historians and Historical Writing*, ed. Kelly Boyd (London: Fitroy Dearborn, 1999), 1295–96; Bert S. Hall, "Lynn Townsend White, Jr. (1907–1987)," *Technology and Culture* 30 (January 1989): 194–213; Hall, "Lynn White's *Medieval Technology and Social*

Change After Thirty Years," in *Technical Change: Methods and Themes in the History of Technology*, ed. Robert Fox (London: Harwood, 1996), 85–101; Alex Roland, "Once More into the Stirrups: Lynn White jr., *Medieval Technology and Social Change*," *Technology and Culture* 44 (July 2003): 574–85.

15. Anna Muthesius, *Byzantine Silk Weaving, A.D. 400 to A.D. 1200*, ed. Ewald Kislinger and Johannes Koder (Vienna: Verlag Fassbaender, 1997); Jonathan M. Bloom, *Paper before Print: The History and Impact of Paper in the Islamic World* (New Haven, Conn.: Yale University Press, 2001); Horden and Purcell, *Corrupting Sea*; McCormick, *Origins of the European Economy*.

CHAPTER 1

1. Alexander P. Kazhdan et al., "Byzantium, History of," in *The Oxford Dictionary of Byzantium*, 3 vols., ed. Kazhdan et al. (New York: Oxford University Press, 1991), 1:345–62. For a discussion of the more traditional divisions, see Mango, *Byzantium*, 1–31. For the Arab-Byzantine conflict in the seventh century, see Walter E. Kaegi, *Byzantium and the Early Conquests* (Cambridge: Cambridge University Press, 1992). A broad range of Byzantine topics is treated in Mango, ed., *Oxford History of Byzantium*. Substantial introductions to the entire field are Browning, *Byzantine Empire* and Treadgold, *History of the Byzantine State*.

2. Mango, *Byzantium*, 32–41. For the Byzantine army, see Warren Treadgold, *Byzantium and Its Army, 284–1081* (Stanford, Calif.: Stanford University Press, 1995); Mark C. Bartusis, *The Late Byzantine Army: Arms and Society, 1204–1453* (Philadelphia: University of Pennsylvania Press, 1992); Clive Foss, "Life in the City and the Country," in *Oxford History of Byzantium*, ed. Mango, 71–95.

3. A.H.M. Jones, *The Later Roman Empire, 284–602: A Social, Economic, and Administrative Survey*, 2 vols. (Norman: University of Oklahoma Press, 1964), 2:767–823; Alexander Kazhdan, "The Peasantry," in *The Byzantines*, ed. Guglielmo Cavallo, trans. Thomas Dunlap, Teresa Lavender Fagan, and Charles Lambert (Chicago: University of Chicago Press, 1997), 43–73.

4. Kazhdan, "Peasantry," 50–51.

5. Kazhdan, "Peasantry," 50. A fundamental study of oil presses is A. G. Drachmann, *Ancient Oil Mills and Presses* (Copenhagen: Levin and Munksgaard, 1932); see also Olivier Callot, *Huileries antiques de Syrie du nord* (Paris: Librairie Orientaliste aux Geuthner, 1984).

6. Kazhdan, "Peasantry," 48–49.

7. Kazhdan, "Peasantry." Also, Linda Cheetham, "Threshing and Winnowing—An Ethnographic Study," *Antiquity* 56 (July 1982): 127–30.

8. Kazhdan, "Peasantry"; Alice-Mary Talbot, "Women," in *Byzantines*, ed. Cavallo, 117–43, esp. 126–27.

9. Kazhdan, "Peasantry," 63–67 and Mango, *Byzantium*, 43–46. For longer accounts of changes in the economies of the countryside, see esp. Paul Lemerle, *The Agrarian History of Byzantium from the Origins to the Twelfth Century: The Sources and Problems* (Galway, Ireland: Galway University Press, 1979) and Georg Ostrogorsky, "Agrarian Conditions in the Byzantine Empire in the Middle Ages," in *The Cambridge Economic History of Europe*, vol. 1, *The Agrarian Life of the Middle Ages*, 2d ed., ed. M. M. Postan (Cambridge: Cambridge University Press, 1966), 205–34. For the later empire, see Angeliki E. Laiou-Thomadakis, *Peasant Society in the Late Byzantine Empire: A Social and Demographic Study* (Princeton, N.J.: Princeton University Press, 1977). A synthesis that emphasizes the constancy of small family production through the centuries is Michel Kaplan, "L'économie paysanne dans L'Empire Byzantin du Vème au Xème siècle," *Klio* 68 (1986): 198–232.

10. Alexander P. Kazhdan, "Farmer's Law," in *Oxford Dictionary of Byzantium*, ed. Kazhdan et al., 2:778. See also Walter Ashburner, "The Farmer's Law," *Journal of Hellenic Studies* 32 (1912): 68–95, which includes an English translation of the law, and for a cogent discussion of why it cannot be used to draw general conclusions about Byzantine agriculture, Mark Whittow, *The Making of the Byzantines, 600–1025* (Berkeley and Los Angeles: University of California Press, 1996), 115–16.

11. Mango, *Byzantium*, 60–61; Foss, "Life in City and Country," esp. 71–88.

12. Besim S. Hakim, "Julian of Ascalon's Treatise of Construction and Design Rules from Sixth-Century Palestine," *Journal of the Society of Architectural Historians* 60 (March 2001): 4–25, citation on 4.

13. Clive F. W. Foss and Anthony Cutler, "Cities," in *Oxford Dictionary of Byzantium*, ed. Kazhdan et al., 1:464–66; Mango, *Byzantium*, 60–87; Michael McCormick, "Byzantium and the West, 700–900," in *New Cambridge Medieval History*, ed. McKitterick, 2:349–80, esp. 350–57.

14. Cyril Mango, "Constantinople" and "Constantinople, Monuments of," in *Oxford Dictionary of Byzantium*, ed. Kazhdan et al., 1:508–12 and 516–20; Walter Emil Kaegi, "Nika Revolt," in *Oxford Dictionary of Byzantium*, ed. Kazhdan et al., 3:1473.

15. A. Grabar, "Byzantine Architecture and Art," in *The Cambridge Medieval History*, vol. 4, *The Byzantine Empire*, pt. 2, *Government, Church and Civilisation*, ed. J. M. Hussey (Cambridge: Cambridge University Press, 1967), 306–53, esp. 316–17; Cyril Mango, "Hagia Sophia," in *Oxford Dictionary of Byzantium*, ed. Kazhdan et al., 2:892–95; Richard Krautheimer, *Early Christian and Byzantine Architecture* (Hammondsworth, Middlesex: Penguin Books, 1965), 149–70.

16. For technical accounts of the structure that discusses the many changes made after the time of Justinian, see esp. Rowland J. Mainstone, *Hagia Sophia: Architecture, Structure and Liturgy of Justinian's Great Church* (New York: Thames and Hudson, 1997), citation on 9; Robert Mark and Ahmet S. Çakmak, eds., *Hagia Sophia from the Age of Justinian to the Present* (Cambridge: Cambridge University Press, 1992). See also Robert Mark, *Light, Wind, and Structure: The Mystery of the Master Builders* (Cambridge, Mass.: MIT Press, 1990), 73–89.

17. Robert Ousterhout, *Master Builders of Byzantium* (Princeton, N.J.: Princeton University Press, 1999), 128–37.

18. Ousterhout, *Master Builders*, esp. 58–84.

19. Ousterhout, *Master Builders*, 234–44; André Grabar, *Greek Mosaics of the Byzantine Period* (New York: New American Library, 1964), 5–24.

20. Steven Runciman, "Byzantine Trade and Industry," in *The Cambridge Economic History of Europe*, vol. 2, *Trade and Industry in the Middle Ages*, 2d ed., ed. M. M. Postan and Edward Miller, with the assistance of Cynthia Postan (Cambridge: Cambridge University Press, 1987), 132–67 and 889–92; Nicolas Oikonomidès, "Entrepreneurs," in *Byzantines*, ed. Cavallo, 144–71; and, for coinage, Michael F. Hendy, *Studies in the Byzantine Monetary Economy, c. 300–1450* (Cambridge: Cambridge University Press, 1985), 256–69.

21. Oikonomidès, "Entrepreneurs," esp. 145–50; Alice–Mary Talbot, "Women," esp. 130–31; Alexander P. Kazhdan and Anthony Cutler, "Artisan" and "Artist," in *Oxford Dictionary of Byzantium*, ed. Kazhdan et al., 1:196 and 196–201.

22. Alexander P. Kazhdan, "Guilds," in *Oxford Dictionary of Byzantium*, ed. Kazhdan et al., 2:887; Oikonomidès, "Entrepreneurs," 150–60; Speros Vryonis Jr., "Byzantine *Democratia* and Guilds in the Eleventh Century," *Dumbarton Oaks Papers* 17 (Washington, D.C.: Dumbarton Oaks, 1963), 289–314; and, for an English translation of the *Book of the Eparch*, Edwin Hanson Freshfield, *Roman Law in the Later Roman Empire: Byzantine Guilds, Professional and Commercial* (Cambridge: Cambridge University Press, 1938).

23. Anthony Cutler, *The Hand of the Master: Craftsmanship, Ivory, and Society in Byzantium (9th–11th Centuries)* (Princeton, N.J.: Princeton University Press, 1994), esp. 79–153.

24. Leslie Brubaker and John Haldon, *Byzantium in the Iconoclast Era (c. 680–850): The Sources, An Annotated Survey* (Aldershot: Ashgate, 2001); Anthony Bryer and Judith Herrin, eds., *Iconoclasm: Papers given at the Ninth Spring Symposium of Byzantine Studies* (Birmingham: Centre for Byzantine Studies, University of Birmingham, 1977); Paul A. Hollingsworth and Anthony Cutler, "Iconoclasm," in *Oxford Dictionary of Byzantium*, ed. Kazhdan et al., 2:975–77; Patricia Karlin-Hayter, "Iconoclasm," in *Oxford History of Byzantium*, ed. Mango, 153–62; Mango, *Byzantium*, 98–99 and 256–81; Alexander A. Vasiliev, *History of the Byzantine Empire* (Madison: University of Wisconsin Press, 1952), 251–65 (quotation on 261), and 283–90.

25. A classic study is Robert Sabatino Lopez, "Silk Industry in the Byzantine Empire," *Speculum* 20 (January 1945): 1–42. Fundamental to recent scholarship are the extensive and thoroughgoing studies of Anna Muthesius: *Byzantine Silk Weaving* and *Studies in Byzantine and Islamic Silk Weaving* (London: Pindar Press, 1995), 120–22, for the introduction of sericulture into Byzantium.

26. Muthesius, *Byzantine Silk Weaving*, 5–18 and *Studies*, 122–24.

27. Muthesius, *Byzantine Silk Weaving*, 14–33 and *Studies*, 124–34.

28. Nicolas Oikonomidès, "Silk Trade and Production in Byzantium From the Sixth to the Ninth Century: The Seals of Kommerkiarioi," *Dumbarton Oaks Papers* 40 (1986): 33–53, citation on 50; Treadgold, *Byzantium and Its Army*, 181–86.

CHAPTER 2

1. Donner, *Early Islamic Conquests*, 1–9, provides an excellent summary of historiographic issues. For a short summary of the conquests, see Fred M. Donner, "Islam, Conquests of" and C. E. Bosworth, "Islamic Administration," in *Dictionary of the Middle Ages*, 13 vols., ed. Joseph R. Strayer (New York: Charles Scribner's Sons, 1982–89), 6: 566–74 and 588–92, respectively. See also the relevant chapters of Lapidus, *History of Islamic Societies*.

2. Donner, *Early Islamic Conquests*, 11–15.

3. Richard W. Bulliet, *The Camel and the Wheel* (New York: Columbia University Press, Morningside Edition, 1990), 90–91; Donner, *Early Islamic Conquests*, 18–20.

4. Donner, *Early Islamic Conquests*, 34–37; Lapidus, *History of Islamic Societies*, 14–15 and 18–23.

5. Clifford Edmund Bosworth, *The New Islamic Dynasties: A Chronological and Genealogical Manual* (New York: Columbia University Press, 1996); Kaegi, *Byzantium and the Early Islamic Conquests*; Lapidus, *History of Islamic Societies*, 31–44; see also Richard W. Bulliet, *Conversion to Islam in the Medieval Period: An Essay in Quantitative History* (Cambridge, Mass.: Harvard University Press, 1979).

6. A. L. Udovitch, "Introduction: Technology, Land Tenure, and Rural Society: Aspects of Continuity in the Agricultural History of the Pre-Modern Middle East," in *The Islamic Middle East, 700–1900*, ed. Udovitch (Princeton, N.J.: The Darwin Press, 1981), 11–26; Michael G. Morony, "Landholding in Seventh-Century Iraq: Late Sasanian and Early Islamic Patterns," in *Islamic Middle East*, ed. Udovitch, 135–75.

7. Morony, "Landholding," 162–75.

8. A.K.S. Lambton, "Reflections on the Role of Agriculture in Medieval Persia," in *Islamic Middle East*, ed. Udovitch, 283–312; Ira M. Lapidus, "Arab Settlement and Economic Development of Iraq and Iran in the Age of the Umayyad and Early Abbasid Caliphs," in *Islamic Middle East*, ed. Udovitch, 177–207; Donald R. Hill, *Islamic Science and Engineering* (Edinburgh: Edinburgh University Press, 1993), 181–83; A.K.S. Lambton et al., "Kanat," in *The Encyclopaedia of Islam*, new ed., 11 vols., ed. P. J. Bearman et al. (Leiden: E. J. Brill, 1978–2001), 4:528–33.

9. Lapidus, "Arab Settlement," 177–207.

10. Hassanein Rabie, "Some Technical Aspects of Agriculture in Medieval Egypt," in *Islamic Middle East*, ed. Udovitch, 59–89; see also Sato Tsugitaka, *State and Rural Society in Medieval Islam: Sultans, Muqtas and Fallahun* (Leiden: E.J. Brill, 1997), 177–233, for a study of Egyptian rural society from the twelfth century to the fourteenth.

11. Almad Y. al-Hassan and Donald R. Hill, *Islamic Technology: An Illustrated History* (Cambridge: Cambridge University Press, and Paris: UNESCO, 1986), 36–42; Thomas F. Glick, *Islamic and Christian Spain in the Early Middle Ages* (Princeton, N.J.: Princeton University Press, 1979), 235–38; Hill, *Islamic Science and Engineering*, 94–95; Thorkild Schiøler, *Roman and Islamic Water-Lifting Wheels* (Odense: Odense Universitetsforlag, 1973).

12. Glick, *Islamic and Christian Spain*, 27–30, 51–109.

13. Thomas F. Glick, "Irrigation and Hydraulic Technology in Islamic Spain: Methodological Considerations," in *Irrigation and Hydraulic Technology: Medieval Spain and Its Legacy* (Aldershot: Variorum, Ashgate, 1996), 1:1–20;

Glick, *Irrigation and Society in Medieval Valencia* (Cambridge, Mass.: Belknap Press of Harvard University Press, 1970), 177–84; Glick, *Islamic and Christian Spain*, 68–76; Maya Shatzmiller, *Labour in the Medieval Islamic World* (Leiden: E. J. Brill, 1994), 183–86, for a discussion of irrigation throughout the Islamic world.

14. Glick, *Islamic and Christian Spain*, 76–109; Andrew M. Watson, "A Medieval Green Revolution: New Crops and Farming Techniques in the Early Islamic World," in *Islamic Middle East*, ed. Udovitch, 29–58, for a synopsis; Andrew M. Watson, *Agricultural Innovation in the Early Islamic World: The Diffusion of Crops and Farming Techniques, 700–1100* (Cambridge: Cambridge University Press, 1983).

15. Watson, "Medieval Green Revolution" and *Agricultural Innovation*.

16. Ernst J. Grube, "What is Islamic Architecture?" in *Architecture of the Islamic World: Its History and Social Meaning,* ed. George Michell (London: Thames and Hudson, 1978), 10–14 and Robert Hillenbrand, *Islamic Art and Architecture* (London: Thames and Hudson 1999). Standard introductions to medieval Islamic architecture include K.A.C. Creswell, *A Short Account of Early Muslim Architecture*, rev. and supplemented by James W. Allan (Aldershot: Scolar Press, 1989); Richard Ettinghausen and Oleg Grabar, *The Art and Architecture of Islam, 650–1250* (New Haven, Conn.: Yale University Press, 1987). For short summaries, see Susan L. Douglass, *World Eras*, vol. 2, *Rise and Spread of Islam, 622–1500* (Detroit: Gale, 2002), 107–10 and Andrew Petersen, *Dictionary of Islamic Architecture* (London: Routledge, 1996), under alphabetically arranged headwords ("Iwan," 130).

17. Douglass, *World Eras,* 2:109.

18. Grube, "What is Islamic Architecture?" 12–14.

19. For concise summaries, see Douglass, *World Eras*, 2:105–19 and Petersen, *Dictionary of Islamic Architecture*, under alphabetically arranged headwords (e.g., "minaret"). See also Martin Frishman, "Islam and the Form of the Mosque," in *The Mosque: History, Architectural Development and Regional Diversity*, ed. Martin Frishman and Hassan-Uddin Khan (London: Thames and Hudson, 1994), 17–41. For an in-depth study, see Finbarr Barry Flood, *The Great Mosque of Damascus: Studies on the Making of Umayyad Visual Culture* (Leiden: Brill, 2001); see also Ronald Lewcock, "Materials and Techniques," in *Architecture of the Islamic World*, ed. Michell, 129–43, esp. 133–34; Glick, *Islamic and Christian Spain*, 224–26; Glick, "Muhtasib and Mustasaf: A Case Study of Institutional Diffusion," *Viator* 2 (1971): 59–81.

110

20. Lewcock, "Materials and Techniques," 134–36.

21. Lewcock, "Materials and Techniques," 136–37.

22. Lewcock, "Materials and Techniques," 137–38 and Glick, *Islamic and Christian Spain*, 224–25.

23. Lewcock, "Materials and Techniques," 136 and 141–42.

24. Bulliet, *Camel and the Wheel*, esp. 223–30; Hugh Kennedy, "From *Polis* to *Madina*: Urban Change in Late Antique and Early Islamic Syria," *Past and Present* 106 (February 1985): 3–27. See also Nikita Elisséeff, "Physical Layout," in R. B. Serjeant, ed., *The Islamic City* (Paris: UNESCO, 1980), 90–103 and A. H. Hourani and S. M. Stern, eds., *The Islamic City: A Colloquium* (Philadelphia: University of Pennsylvania Press, 1970). For a recent study of a single city, see Chase F. Robinson, ed., *A Medieval Islamic City Reconsidered: An Interdisciplinary Approach to Samarra* (Oxford: Oxford University Press, 2001).

25. See esp. Jonathan Bloom and Sheila Blair, *Islamic Arts* (New York: Phaidon Press, 1997), 81–86 and Ettinghausen and Grabar, *Art and Architecture of Islam*; see also al-Hassan and Hill, *Islamic Technology*, 178–90. A fundamental work of scholarship for textile studies is R. B. Serjeant, *Islamic Textiles: Material for a History up to the Mongol Conquest* (Beirut: Librairie du Liban, 1972).

26. E. Ashtor, "Kattan," in *Encyclopaedia of Islam*, ed. Bearman et al., 4:774.

27. al-Hassan and Hill, *Islamic Technology*, 180–81; Bloom and Blair, *Islamic Arts*, 86–87.

28. E. Ashtor, "Kutn, Kutun (A.), cotton, I: In the mediaeval Arab and Persian Lands," in *Encyclopaedia of Islam*, ed. Bearman et al., 5:554–57; Bloom and Blair, *Islamic Arts*, 88; al-Hassan and Hill, *Islamic Technology*, 179–90, and for paper, 190–97; Carl Johan Lamm, *Cotton in Medieval Textiles in the Near East* (Paris: Libraire Orientaliste Paul Geuthner, 1937); Watson, *Agricultural Innovation*, 31–41.

29. Bloom and Blair, *Islamic Arts*, 88, 227, 230–31; al-Hassan and Hill, *Islamic Technology*, 179–90.

30. Baker, *Islamic Textiles*, esp. 53–63; Bloom and Blair, *Islamic Arts*, 93–96; Hillenbrand, *Islamic Art and Architecture*, 49–50.

31. Bloom and Blair, *Islamic Arts*, 100–27.

32. Bloom and Blair, *Islamic Arts*, 100–27; al-Hassan and Hill, *Islamic Technology*, 160–70; Venetia Porter, *Islamic Tiles* (New York: Interlink Books, 1995), esp. 8–10.

33. Bloom and Blair, *Islamic Arts*, 113–23 and 257–64; and Rachel Ward, *Islamic Metalwork* (New York: Thames and Hudson, 1993), esp. 9–37.

34. S. D. Goitein, *A Mediterranean Society: The Jewish Communities of the Arab World as Portrayed in the Documents of the Cairo Geniza*, vol. 1, *Economic Foundations* (Berkeley and Los Angeles: University of California Press, 1967–93), esp. 1–28, which contains a detailed account of the discovery and the subsequent destinations of the documents. On Goitein, see Glick, "S. D. Goitein," in *Encyclopedia of Historians*, ed. Boyd, 473.

35. Goitein, *Mediterranean Society*, 1:80–90.

36. Goitein, *Mediterranean Society*, 1:91–100.

37. Shatzmiller, *Labour*.

38. Shatzmiller, *Labour*, 348–50.

39. Shatzmiller, *Labour*, 347–52 and 358–59; see also Goitein, *Mediterranean Society*, 1:127–31.

40. Shatzmiller, *Labour*, 352–57.

41. Shatzmiller, *Labour*, 369–97, for a discussion that examines materials through the fourteenth century.

42. See esp. Dimitri Gutas, *Greek Thought, Arabic Culture: The Graeco-Arabic Translation Movement in Baghdad and early Abbasid Society (2nd–4th/8th–10th Centuries)* (London: Routledge, 1998) and A. I. Sabra, "The Appropriation and Subsequent Naturalization of Greek Science in Medieval Islam: A Preliminary Statement," in *Tradition, Transmission, Transformation: Proceedings of Two Conferences on Pre-Modern Science Held at the University of Oklahoma*, ed. F. Jamil Ragep and Sally P. Ragep with Steven Livesey (Leiden: E. J. Brill, 1996), 3–27. See also Ahmad Dallal, "Science, Medicine, and Technology: The Making of a Scientific Culture," in *The Oxford History of Islam*, ed. John L. Esposito (Oxford: Oxford University Press, 1999), 155–213; Hill, *Islamic Science and Engineering*, 9–14; George Saliba, "The Function of Mechanical Devices in Medieval Islamic Society," in *Science and Technology in Medieval Society*, Annals of the New York Academy of Sciences 441, ed. Pamela O. Long (New York: New York Academy of Sciences, 1985): 141–51.

43. Donald Hill, *A History of Engineering in Classical and Medieval Times* (London: Routledge, 1996), 202–03; and, for the treatise, Banu (Sons of) Musa bin Shakir, *The Book of Ingenious Devices*, trans. Donald R. Hill (Reidel: Dordrecht, 1979).

44. Hill, *History of Engineering*, 60–62; al-Hassan and Hill, *Islamic Technology*, 60–62; Banu Musa, *Book of Ingenious Devices*.

45. Ibn al-Razzaz al-Jazari, *The Book of Knowledge of Ingenious Mechanical Devices*, trans. Donald R. Hill (Reidel: Dordrecht, 1974). For discussions of this work, see al-Hassan and Hill, *Islamic Technology*, esp. 42–49 and 58–59 (citation); Hill, *History of Engineering*, 146–52; Hill, *Islamic Science and Engineering*, 97–105 and 124–35; Saliba, "Function of Mechanical Devices."

46. Al-Hassan and Hill, *Islamic Technology*, 57 and 64–65; Hill, *Islamic Science and Engineering*, 60–70. See also E. Wiedmann, "al-Mizan," in *Encyclopaedia of Islam*, ed. Bearman et al., 8:195–204.

47. Silke Ackermann, "Astrolabe," http://www.mhs.ox.ac.uk/EPACT/article.asp?article=astrolabe, citation on 1. See also Sharon Gibbs and George Saliba, *Planispheric Astrolabes from the National Museum of American History* (Washington, D.C.: Smithsonian Institution Press, 1984), esp. 1–11, which contains a detailed explanation of the astrolabe; al-Hassan and Hill, *Islamic Technology*, 66–67; Hill, *Islamic Science and Engineering*, 48–57; David A. King, "Astronomical Instrumentation in the Medieval Near East," in *Islamic Astronomical Instruments* (London: Variorum Reprints, 1987), I; David A. King and George Saliba, eds., *From Deferent to Equant: A Volume of Studies in the History of Science in the Ancient and Medieval Near East in Honor of E. S. Kennedy* (New York: New York Academy of Sciences, 1987).

CHAPTER 3

1. For the Barbarians, see esp. Walter A. Goffart, *Barbarians and Romans, A.D. 418–584* (Princeton, N.J: Princeton University Press, 1980) and J. M. Wallace-Hadrill, *The Barbarian West, 400–1000*, rev. ed. (Oxford: Basil Blackwell, 1996). For an insightful discussion of the transition from late Roman to early medieval forms in one region, the Iberian Peninsula, which emphasizes how little is actually known, see Thomas F. Glick, *From Muslim Fortress to Christian Castle: Social and Cultural Change in Medieval Spain* (Manchester: Manchester University Press, 1995), 3–12. For a recent essay which pays due appreciation to the complexities and uncertainties of the early medieval social order, see Hans-Werner Goetz, "Social and Military Institutions," in *New Cambridge Medieval History*, ed. McKitterick, 2:451–80. A richly detailed chronological account of medieval Britain emphasizing economic issues is Christopher Dyer, *Making a Living in the Middle Ages: The People of Britain, 850–1520* (New Haven, Conn.: Yale University Press, 2002). A good introductory account that includes the history of technology is Steven A. Walton and Bert S. Hall, "Science, Technology, and Health," in *World Eras*, vol. 4, *Medieval Europe, 814–1350*, ed. Jeremiah Hackett (Detroit, Mich.: Gale Group, 2002), 431–77.

2. Thorough treatments of medieval rural life can be found in Georges Duby, *Rural Economy and Country Life in the Medieval West*, trans. Cynthia Postan (Columbia: University of South Carolina Press, 1968); Postan, ed., *Agrarian Life of the Middle Ages*. An interdisciplinary study of the medieval village and its structures by an archaeologist and a historian is Jean Chapelot and Robert Fossier, *The Village and the House in the Middle Ages*, trans. Henry Cleere (Berkeley and Los Angeles: University of California Press, 1985).

3. For the Carolingian period, see Adriaan Verhulst, *The Carolingian Economy* (Cambridge: Cambridge University Press, 2002), 31–71. See also Robert Fossier, *Peasant Life in the Medieval West*, trans. Juliet Vale (Oxford: Basil Blackwell, 1988), 86–125; Frances Gies and Joseph Gies, *Cathedral, Forge, and Waterwheel: Technology and Invention in the Middle Ages* (New York: HarperCollins, 1994), 44–45; White, *Medieval Technology and Social Change*, 39–78.

4. White, *Medieval Technology and Social Change*, 39–78.

5. Karl Brunner, "Continuity and Discontinuity of Roman Agricultural Knowledge in the Early Middle Ages," in *Agriculture in the Middle Ages: Technology, Practice, and Representation*, ed. Del Sweeney (Philadelphia: University of Pennsylvania Press, 1995), 21–49; Joachim Henning, *Südosteuropa zwischen Antike und Mittelalter: Archäologische Beiträge zur Landwirtschaft del I. Jahrtausends u.Z.* (Berlin: Akademie Verlag, 1987). See also Fossier, *Peasant Life*, 97–99; Werner Rösener, *Peasants in the Middle Ages*, trans. Alexander Stützer (Urbana: University of Illinois Press, 1992), 108–17; Michael Toch, "Agricultural Progress and Agricultural Technology in Medieval Germany: An Alternative Model," in *Technology and Resource Use in Medieval Europe: Cathedrals, Mills, and Mines*, ed. Elizabeth Bradford Smith and Michael Wolfe (Aldershot: Ashgate, 1997), 158–69; Georges Comet, "Technology and Agricultural Expansion in the Middle Ages: The Example of France North of the Loire" and Georges Raepsaet, "The Development of Farming Implements Between the Seine and the Rhine from the Second to the Twelfth Centuries," in *Medieval Farming and Technology: The Impact of Agricultural Change in Northwest Europe*, ed. Grenville Astill and John Langdon (Leiden: Brill, 1997), 11–39 and 40–68, respectively; Comet, *Le paysan et son outile: Essai d'histoire technique des cereals (France, VIIIe–XVe siècle)* (Rome: École Française de Rome, 1992).

6. Morris Bishop, *The Middle Ages* (New York: Houghton Mifflin, 2001), 208–35; Hans-Werner Goetz, *Life in the Middle Ages from the Seventh to the Thirteenth Century*, ed. Steven Rowan, trans. Albert Wimmer (Notre Dame:

University of Notre Dame Press, 1993), 143–44. For the importance of gardens and the intense care that they required, see especially Paolo Squatriti, *Water and Society in Early Medieval Italy, A.D. 400–1000* (Cambridge: Cambridge University Press, 1998), 80–86.

7. As Robert Fossier noted, "whatever the preoccupation of individual historians, almost all the observations which one can make ... point to the tenth century as the age of growth." See Fossier, "Rural Economy and Country Life," in *New Cambridge Medieval History*, ed. Reuter, 3:27–63 and 740–42, citation on 27. See also John Langdon, Grenville Astill, and Jankin Myrdal, introduction to *Medieval Farming and Technology*, 1–9.

8. Duby, *Rural Economy*, 94–99; Adriaan Verhulst, "Economic Organisation," in *New Cambridge Medieval History*, ed. McKitterick, 2:481–509; Charles Parain, "The Evolution of Agricultural Technique," in *Cambridge Economic History*, ed. Postan, 1:125–79; Chapelot and Fossier, *Village and the House*. A detailed examination of crop rotation in one region (Flanders) underscores the complexity of the issue: Erik Thoen, "The Birth of 'The Flemish Husbandry': Agricultural Technology in Medieval Flanders," in *Medieval Farming and Technology*, ed. Astill and Langdon, 69–88, esp. 74–77. See also Rösener, *Peasants*, 117–21 and 126–32.

9. For a succinct summary of the controversy over the horse collar, see Paul J. Gans, "The Medieval Technology Pages: The Great Harness Controversy" at http://scholar.chem.nyu.edu/tekpages/texts/harncont.html. See also Duby, *Rural Economy*, 109–12; Parain, "Evolution of Agricultural Techniques," 140–51; White, *Medieval Technology and Social Change*, 57–69; Goetz, *Life in the Middle Ages*, 140–51. For a discussion of the interrelated technologies that accompanied the horse as a draft animal, see esp. John Langdon, *Horses, Oxen, and Technological Innovation: The Use of Draught Animals in English Farming from 1066 to 1550* (Cambridge: Cambridge University Press, 1986), 4–21; and, for Flanders, see Thoen, "Birth of 'The Flemish Husbandry,'" 81 and Rösener, *Peasants*, 111–14.

10. A basic treatment of the manor is Duby, *Rural Economy*, 28–58. For more recent discussions, see Verhulst, "Economic Organisation," 488–99; Verhulst, *Carolingian Economy*, 33–52; Goetz, "Social and Military Institutions," esp. 474–76; Rösener, *Peasants*, esp. 211–18; and, for "free" peasants, 224–36.

11. Goetz, *Life in the Middle Ages*, 140–51; Fossier, *Peasant Life*, 17–20 and 31–33; Barbara A. Hanawalt, *The Ties that Bound: Peasant Families in Medieval England* (New York: Oxford University Press, 1986), 141–55; Hanawalt, "Peasant Women's Contribution to the Home Economy in Late Medieval England," in *Women and Work in Preindustrial Europe*, ed. Hanawalt (Bloomington: Indiana University Press, 1986), 3–19.

12. On land clearance, see esp. Duby, *Rural Economy*, 65–87; Fossier, *Peasant Life*, 104–12; and, more generally, Verhulst, "Economic Organisation," esp. 481–83. For the Netherlands, see Peter Hoppenbrouwers, "Agricultural Production and Technology in the Netherlands, c. 1000–1500," in *Medieval Farming and Technology*, ed. Astill and Langdon, 89–114, esp. 96–101.

13. Squatriti, *Water and Society*, 67–76 (citation on 74) and 97–125.

14. Thoen, "Birth of 'The Flemish Husbandry,'" 83–84; Bjørn Poulsen, "Agricultural Technology in Medieval Denmark" and Janken Myrdal, "The Agricultural Transformation of Sweden, 1000–1300," in *Medieval Farming and Technology*, ed. Astill and Langdon, 114–45 and 147–71, respectively.

15. Constance Hoffman Berman, *Medieval Agriculture, the Southern French Countryside, and the Early Cistercians. A Study of Forty-three Monasteries, Transactions of the American Philosophical Society* 76:5 (Philadelphia: American Philosophical Society, 1986), esp. 11–30 and 61–93. See also Berman, *The Cistercian Evolution: The Invention of a Religious Order in Twelfth-Century Europe* (Philadelphia: University of Pennsylvania Press, 2000), who argues that the traditional foundation date of the Cistercians (1098) should be revised to the mid-twelfth century.

16. Berman, *Medieval Agriculture*, 94–117.

17. Bloch, "Advent and Triumph of the Watermill." For an excellent summary and critique of Bloch's essay, see Paolo Squatriti, "'Advent and Conquests' of the Water Mill in Italy," in *Technology and Resource Use*, ed. Smith and Wolfe, 125–38. For Roman technology, see esp. Örjan Wikander, *Exploitation of Water-Power or Technological Stagnation? A Reappraisal of the Productive Forces in the Roman Empire* (Lund: C.W. K. Gleerup, 1984); Wikander, ed., *Handbook of Ancient Water Technology* (Leiden: Brill, 2000); Kevin Greene, "Perspectives on Roman Technology," *Oxford Journal of Archaeology* 9 (1990): 209–19; Greene, "Technological Innovation and Economic Progress in the Ancient World: M. I. Finley Reconsidered," *Economic History Review* 53 (2000): 29–59. For the view of the mill as a sign of a medieval industrial revolution, see esp. White, *Medieval Technology and Social Change*, 79–103; Jean Gimpel, *The Medieval Machine: The Industrial Revolution of the Middle Ages* (Hammondsworth, Middlesex: Penguin Books, 1976); Terry Reynolds, *Stronger than a Hundred Men: A History of the Vertical Water Wheel* (Baltimore, Md.: Johns Hopkins University Press, 1983). For recent dissents from this point of view, see esp. Richard Holt, "Mechanization and the Medieval English Economy," in *Technology and Resource Use*, ed. Smith and Wolfe, 139–57; Richard Holt, *The Mills of Medieval England* (Oxford: Basil Blackwell, 1988); Adam Lucas, *Wind, Water, Work: Milling Technology in the Ancient and Medieval Worlds* (Leiden: Brill, forthcoming).

18. See Hill, *History of Engineering*, 155–58; Bradford B. Blaine, "Mills," in *Dictionary of the Middle Ages*, ed. Strayer, 8:389–95, esp. 390–91; Glick, *From Muslim Fortress to Christian Castle*, 115–22; Squatriti, *Water and Society*, 130–32.

19. Hill, *History of Engineering*, 155–79; Bloch, "Advent and Triumph of the Watermill," 137–68; Squatriti, "'Advent and Conquests,'" esp. 136–38; Squatriti, *Water and Society*, 126–59; Holt, *Mills of Medieval England*, 117–44; John Muendel, "The Horizontal Mills of Medieval Pistoia," *Technology and Culture* 15 (January 1974): 194–225; Muendel, "The Internal Functions of a 14th-Century Florentine Flour Factory," *Technology and Culture* 32 (July 1991): 498–520.

20. David Crossley, "The Archaeology of Water Power in Britain Before the Industrial Revolution," in *Technology and Resource Use*, ed. Smith and Wolfe, 109–24; Holt, *Mills of Medieval England*, 17–35.

21. Holt, "Mechanization," 139–57, citation on 145; Richard L. Hills, *Power from the Wind: A History of Windmill Technology* (Cambridge: Cambridge University Press, 1994), 25–49; White, *Medieval Technology and Social Change*, 87–88.

22. Holt, "Mechanization," 149–157; Gies and Gies, *Cathedral, Forge, and Waterwheel*, esp. 114–18.

23. See esp. Bartlett, *Making of Europe*, 64–70; Goetz, *Life in the Middle Ages*, 167–73; Kelly DeVries, *Medieval Military Technology* (Peterborough, Ontario: Broadview Press, 1992), esp. 202–49; Charles Coulson, *Castles in Medieval Society: Fortresses in England, France, and Ireland in the Central Middle Ages* (Oxford: Oxford University Press, 2003); M. W. Thompson, *The Rise of the Castle* (Cambridge: Cambridge University Press, 1991); Philip Warner, *The Medieval Castle: Life in a Fortress in Peace and War* (London: Penguin, 2001) .

24. DeVries, *Medieval Military Technology*, 202–12. See also Thompson, *Rise of the Castle* and Warner, *Medieval Castle*, 29–46.

25. DeVries, *Medieval Military Technology*, 204–08.

26. DeVries, *Medieval Military Technology,* esp. 213–35; Thompson, *Rise of the Castle*; Warner, *Medieval Castle*, esp. 187–217.

27. Pierre Toubert, *Les structures du Latium médiéval* (Rome: École Française de Rome, 1973); Pierre Guichard, *Al-Andalus: Estructura antropológica de una sociedad islámica en occidente* (Barcelona: Barral, 1976); Glick, *From Muslim Fortress to Christian Castle*, esp. xi–xxi and 92–124. See also Glick, "Pierre Guichard," in *Encyclopedia of Historians*, ed. Boyd, 496–98.

28. See Fossier, *Peasant Life*, esp. 8–15; Goetz, *Life in the Middle Ages*, 197–236; Richard Hodges and Brian Hobley, eds., *The Rebirth of Towns in the West, A.D. 700–1050* (London: Council for British Archaeology, 1988); David Nicholas, *The Growth of the Medieval City: From Late Antiquity to the Early Fourteenth Century* (London: Longman, 1997). For Britain, see Richard Holt and Gervase Rosser, *The English Medieval Town: A Reader in English Urban History, 1200–1540* (London: Longman, 1990); Dyer, *Making a Living*, 187–227; D. M. Palliser, ed., *The Cambridge Urban History of Britain*, vol. 1, *600–1540* (Cambridge: Cambridge University Press, 2000).

29. Goetz, *Life in the Middle Ages*, esp. 200–10.

30. See Bishop, *Middle Ages*, 176–207; and, in a more complicated picture, Goetz, *Life in the Middle Ages*, 198–210. For Venice and its growing Mediterranean trade, see Frederic C. Lane, *Venice: A Maritime Republic* (Baltimore, Md.: Johns Hopkins University Press, 1973), esp. 1–101. See also McCormick, *Origins of the European Economy*.

31. Steven A. Epstein, "Urban Society," in *The New Cambridge Medieval History*, vol. 5, *c. 1198–c. 1300*, ed. David Abulafia (Cambridge: Cambridge University Press, 1999), 26–37, citation on 31; S. R. Epstein, "Craft Guilds, Apprenticeship, and Technological Change in Preindustrial Europe," *Journal of Economic History* 58 (September 1998): 684–713. The towns of Britain have been well studied; see note 28 above and also Edward Miller and John Hatcher, *Medieval England: Towns, Commerce and Crafts, 1086–1348* (London: Longman, 1995).

32. Epstein, "Urban Society," 26–37; Steven A. Epstein, *Wage Labor and Guilds in Medieval Europe* (Chapel Hill: University of North Carolina Press, 1991); Verhulst, *Carolingian Economy*, 72–74.

33. Theophilus, *The Various Arts: De Diversis Artibus*, ed. and trans. C. R. Dodwell (1961; reprint, Oxford: Clarendon, 1986) and *On Diverse Arts,* ed. and trans. John G. Hawthorne and Cyril S. Smith (1953; reprint, New York: Dover, 1979). For further bibliography and discussion, see Pamela O. Long, *Openness, Secrecy, Authorship: Technical Arts and the Culture of Knowledge from Antiquity to the Renaissance* (Baltimore, Md.: Johns Hopkins University Press, 2001), 85–88.

34. See articles on particular crafts in the Strayer, ed., *Dictionary of the Middle Ages* and in Jane Turner, ed., *The Dictionary of Art*, 34 vols. (New York: Grove's Dictionaries, 1996), which provides detailed technical articles on some of the crafts. For urban crafts in Britain, see Dyer, *Making a Living*, 201–18 and

Miller and Hatcher, *Medieval England*, 51–134. Comprehensive accounts of the technologies of particular crafts are found in John Blair and Nigel Ramsay, eds., *English Medieval Industries: Craftsmen, Techniques, Products* (London: Hambledon Press, 1991). See also D. W. Crossley, *Medieval Industry* (London: Council for British Archeology, 1981) and Heather Swanson, *Medieval Artisans: An Urban Class in Late Medieval England* (Oxford: Basil Blackwell, 1989).

35. John H. Munro, "Textile Technology," in *Dictionary of the Middle Ages*, ed. Strayer, 11:693–711; see also Munro, *Textiles, Towns and Trade: Essays in the Economic History of Late-Medieval England and the Low Countries* (Aldershot: Variorum, Ashgate, 1994); N. B. Harte and K. G. Ponting, eds., *Cloth and Clothing in Medieval Europe: Essays in Memory of Professor E. M. Carus-Wilson* (London: Heinemann Educational Books, 1983); Penelope Walton, "Textiles," in *English Medieval Industries*, ed. Blair and Ramsay, 332–37; Miller and Hatcher, *Medieval England*, 93–127. David Jenkins, ed., *The Cambridge History of Western Textiles*, 2 vols. (New York: Cambridge University Press, 2003), although not published in time to be used here, promises important articles on medieval textiles.

36. For building crafts in England, see Miller and Hatcher, *Medieval England*, 85–93 and the classic work by L. F. Salzman, *Building in England Down to 1540: A Documentary History* (Oxford: Clarendon Press, 1952). For a general introduction to the Romanesque, see Nikolaus Pevsner, *An Outline of European Architecture*, 7th ed. (Harmondsworth: Penguin Books, 1975), 56–88; see also Eric Fernie, "Romanesque: II: Architecture," in *Dictionary of Art*, ed. Turner, 26:568–94.

37. Peter Kidson, Michael T. Davis, and Paul Crossley, "Gothic: II: Architecture," in *Dictionary of Art*, ed. Turner, 13:35–71; John Fitchen, *The Construction of Gothic Cathedrals: A Study in Medieval Vault Erection* (Chicago: University of Chicago Press, 1961); Robert Mark, *Light, Wind, and Structure* and *Experiments in Gothic Structure* (Cambridge, Mass.: MIT Press, 1982); Pevsner, *Outline*, 88–172. See also Lynn T. Courtenay, ed., *The Engineering of Medieval Cathedrals* (Aldershot: Ashgate, 1997) and Nancy Y. Wu, ed., *Ad Quadratum: The Practical Application of Geometry in Medieval Architecture* (Aldershot: Ashgate, 2002).

38. Robert Mark, "Technological Innovation in High Gothic Architecture," in *Technology and Resource Use*, ed. Smith and Wolfe, 11–25, citation on 13; Lon R. Shelby, "Mason: IV: Techniques," in *Dictionary of Art*, ed. Turner, 20:563–66.

39. Lon R. Shelby, "Mason: II: The Masons" and "III: Lodge Organization," in *Dictionary of Art*, ed. Turner, 20:559–63.

40. Shelby, "Mason: II" and "Mason: III."

41 Birgit van den Hoven, *Work in Ancient and Medieval Thought: Ancient Philosophers, Medieval Monks and Theologians and Their Concept of Work, Occupations, and Technology* (Amsterdam: J. C. Gieben, 1996); Jacques Le Goff, *Time, Work, and Culture in the Middle Ages*, trans. Arthur Goldhammer (Chicago: University of Chicago Press, 1980); Long, *Openness, Secrecy, Authorship*, 72–101; George Ovitt Jr., *The Restoration of Perfection: Labor and Technology in Medieval Culture* (New Brunswick, N.J.: Rutgers University Press, 1987).

42. Jerome Taylor, ed. and trans., *The Didascalicon of Hugh of St. Victor* (New York: Columbia University Press, 1961). See also Elspeth Whitney, *Paradise Restored: The Mechanical Arts from Antiquity through the Thirteenth Century*, Transactions of the American Philosophical Society 90:1 (Philadelphia: American Philosophical Society, 1990).

43. David Herlihy, *Opera Muliebria: Women and Work in Medieval Europe* (Philadelphia: Temple University Press, 1990), 75–102; David F. Noble, *A World without Women: The Christian Clerical Culture of Western Science* (New York: Alfred A. Knopf, 1992).

44. Herlihy, *Opera Muliebria*, 127–48, esp. 142–48.

45. Judith M. Bennett, *Ale, Beer, and the Brewster in England: Women's Work in a Changing World, 1300–1600* (Oxford: Oxford University Press, 1996); Bennett, "The Village Ale-Wife: Women and Brewing in Fourteenth-Century England," in *Women and Work*, ed. Hanawalt, 21–36.

46. Kathryn L. Reyerson, "Women in Business in Medieval Montpellier" and Maryanne Kowaleski, "Women's Work in a Market Town: Exeter in the Late Fourteenth Century," in *Women and Work*, ed. Hanawalt, 117–44 and 145–64, respectively.

CHAPTER 4

1 John Haldon, *Warfare, State and Society in the Byzantine World* (London: UCL Press, 1999), 234–79 and Christopher Allmand, "War and the Non-Combatant in the Middle Ages," in *Medieval Warfare: A History*, ed. Maurice Keen (Oxford: Oxford University Press, 1999), 253–72.

2. Maurice Keen, "Introduction: Warfare and the Middle Ages," in *Medieval Warfare*, ed. Keen, 1–9, esp. 9; see also Treadgold, *Byzantium and Its Army*.

3. David Nicole, *Medieval Warfare Source Book: Christian Europe and Its Neighbors* (London: Brockhampton Press, 1998), 15–16.

4. Bulliet, *Camel and the Wheel*, 87–110.

5. Bulliet, *Camel and the Wheel*, 96–100.

6. Donner, "Islam, Conquests of," 6:566–74; Donner, *Early Islamic Conquests*; Nicole, *Medieval Warfare Source Book*, 16–17.

7. Donner, "Islam, Conquests of"; Derek Kennet, "The Form of the Military Cantonments at Samarra: The Organisation of the Abbasid Army" and Jeremy Johns, "Feeding the Army," in *Medieval Islamic City Reconsidered,* ed. Robinson, 157–82 and 183–90, respectively; Nicole, *Medieval Warfare Source Book*, 55–56 and 61–62.

8. Tsugitaka, *State and Rural Society*; Nicole, *Medieval Warfare Source Book*, 62.

9. McCormick, "Byzantium and the West," esp. 353–54; Treadgold, *Byzantium and Its Army*, esp. 98–109 and 187–219.

10. Bernard S. Bachrach, *Merovingian Military Organization, 481–751* (Minneapolis: University of Minnesota Press, 1972); Bachrach, *Early Carolingian Warfare: Prelude to Empire* (Philadelphia: University of Pennsylvania Press, 2001); Philippe Contamine, *War in the Middle Ages*, trans. Michael Jones (Oxford: Basil Blackwell, 1984), 3–29; Timothy Reuter, "Carolingian and Ottonian Warfare," in *Medieval Warfare*, ed. Keen, 13–35.

11. Jim Bradbury, *The Medieval Archer* (New York: St. Martin's Press, 1985), 12–14; DeVries, *Medieval Military Technology*, 32–33; Nicole, *Medieval Warfare Source Book*, 34–37.

12. Josef Alm, *European Crossbows: A Survey*, ed. Guy M. Wilson, trans. Bartlett Wells (Leeds: Royal Armouries Museum, 1994); Bradbury, *Medieval Archer*, 8–10; George T. Dennis, "Flies, Mice, and the Byzantine Crossbow," *Byzantine and Modern Greek Studies* 33 (1992): 265–91; DeVries, *Medieval Military Technology*, 39–44; David Nishimura, "Crossbows, Arrow-Guides, and the Solenarion," *Byzantion* 58 (1988): 422–35; Nicole, *Medieval Warfare Source Book*, 73–74; Ralph Payne-Gallwey, *The Book of the Crossbow* (1903; reprint, New York: Dover Publications, 1995); Nicole Petrin, "Philological Notes on the Crossbow and Related Missile Weapons," *Greek, Roman and Byzantine Studies* 33 (1992): 265–91.

13. Bradbury, *Medieval Archer*, 71–115; Robert Hardy, *Longbow: A Social and Military History*, 3d ed. (London: Bois d'Arc Press, 1992); DeVries, *Medieval Military Technology*, 37–39.

14. Nicole, *Medieval Warfare Source Book*, 34–37; Bartlett, *Making of Europe*, 63–64.

15. Robert Elgood, ed., *Islamic Arms and Armour* (London: Scholar Press, 1979); Nicole, *Medieval Warfare Source Book*, 74–80.

16. R.L.S. Bruce-Mitford, *The Sutton Hoo Ship Burial*, vol. 2, *Arms, Armour and Regalia* (London: British Museum Press, 1978), 273–308, 456–81; A. C. Evans, *The Sutton Hoo Ship Burial*, rev. ed. (London: British Museum Press, 1994).

17. Eric McGeer, *Sowing the Dragon's Teeth: Byzantine Warfare in the Tenth Century* (Washington, D.C.: Dumbarton Oaks, 1995), esp. 171–64, which provides a detailed analysis of Byzantine military organization and Byzantine enemies in the tenth century (citation on 171). See also John Haldon, "Strategies of Defence, Problems of Security: The Garrisons of Constantinople in the Middle Byzantine Period," in *Constantinople and Its Hinterland: Papers from the Twenty-Seventh Spring Symposium of Byzantine Studies, Oxford April 1993*, ed. Cyril Mango and Gilbert Drago (Aldershot: Ashgate, 1995); Nicole, *Medieval Warfare Source Book*, 68.

18. Simon Coupland, "Carolingian Arms and Armor in the Ninth Century," *Viator* 21 (1990): 29–50; see also DeVries, *Medieval Military Technology*, 7–122.

19. White, *Medieval Technology and Social Change*, 1–38. DeVries, *Medieval Military Technology*, 95–122, provides an excellent summary of the scholarship, and, for recent reassessments of White's work, see Roland, "Once More into the Stirrups"; and Reuter, "Carolingian and Ottonian Warfare," 13–35, esp. 27–28.

20. White, *Medieval Technology and Social Change*, 1–38.

21. Bernard S. Bachrach, "Charles Martel, Mounted Shock Combat, the Stirrup, and Feudalism," *Studies in Medieval and Renaissance History* 7, ed. William Bowsky (Lincoln: University of Nebraska Press, 1970), 49–75; Bachrach, "Animals and Warfare in Early Medieval Europe," *Settimane di Studio del Centro Italiano di sull'alto Medioevo* 31 (1985): 707–51, both reprinted in Bachrach, *Armies and Politics in the Early Medieval West* (Aldershot: Variorum, Ashgate, 1993). See also Bachrach, *Early Carolingian Warfare*.

22. Andrew Ayton, "Arms, Armour, and Horses," in *Medieval Warfare*, ed. Keen, 188–208, esp. 188. For plate armor, Claude Blair, *European Armour circa 1066–circa 1700* (London: B. T. Batsford, 1958). For the sword in western Europe, Ewart Oakeshott, *The Sword in the Age of Chivalry* (Woodbridge: Boydell Press, 1964); see also Michael Prestwich, *Armies and Warfare in the Middle Ages: The English Experience* (New Haven, Conn.: Yale University Press, 1996), 12–56.

23. Reuter, "Carolingian and Ottonian Warfare," 13–35, citation on 27–28. For a discussion of western military technology that emphasizes the heavily armed knight, see Bartlett, *Making of Europe*, 60–84. For an extensive reexamination of the components of feudalism, see Susan Reynolds, *Fiefs and Vassals: The Medieval Evidence Reinterpreted* (Oxford: Oxford University Press, 1994).

24. For an overview of sources for the Vikings and Viking expansion, see Peter Sawyer, "The Age of the Vikings and Before," in *The Oxford Illustrated History of the Vikings*, ed. Sawyer (Oxford: Oxford University Press, 1977), 1–18. See also H. B. Clarke, "The Vikings," in *Medieval Warfare*, ed. Keen, 36–58, esp. 42–45 and Paddy Griffith, *The Viking Art of War* (London: Greenhill Books, 1995), esp. 13–37.

25. Clarke, "Vikings," 36–58, esp. 42–45; Griffith, *Viking Art of War*, 162–81.

26. Clarke, "Vikings," 52–55.

27. Jan Bill, "Ships and Seamanship," in *Oxford Illustrated History of the Vikings*, ed. Sawyer, 182–201; Clarke, "Vikings," 52–55.

28. Richard C. Jones, "Fortifications and Sieges in Western Europe, c. 800–1450," in *Medieval Warfare*, ed. Keen, 163–85, esp. 174–75; see also Jim Bradbury, *The Medieval Siege* (Woodbridge: Boydell Press, 1992); Ivy A. Corfis and Michael Wolfe, eds., *The Medieval City under Siege* (Woodbridge: Boydell Press, 1995); John France, *Western Warfare in the Age of the Crusades, 1000–1300* (Ithaca, N.Y.: Cornell University Press, 1999), 77–127; Christopher Marshall, *Warfare in the Latin East, 1192–1291* (Cambridge: Cambridge University Press, 1992), 210–56; Nicole, *Medieval Warfare Source Book*, 83–87; Randall Rogers, *Latin Siege Warfare in the Twelfth Century* (Oxford: Clarendon Press, 1992); Denis F. Sullivan, *Siegecraft: Two Tenth-Century Instructional Manuals by "Heron of Byzantium"* (Washington, D.C.: Dumbarton Oaks, 2000).

29. See Rogers, *Latin Siege Warfare*, 251–73, for a lucid historiographic essay on the issue.

30. Paul E. Chevedden, "The Invention of the Counterweight Trebuchet: A Study in Cultural Diffusion," *Dumbarton Oaks Papers* 54, ed. Alice-Mary Talbot (Washington, D.C.: Dumbarton Oaks , 2000), 71–116; see also Bradbury, *Medieval Siege*, 242–81; George T. Dennis, "Byzantine Heavy Artillery: The Helepolis," *Greek, Roman, and Byzantine Studies* 39 (1998): 99–115; Donald R. Hill, "Trebuchets," *Viator* 4 (1973): 99–114, reprinted in Hill, "Studies in Medieval Islamic Technology from Philo to al-Jazari," in *From Alexandria to Diya Bakr*, ed. David A. King (Aldershot: Variorum, Ashgate, 1998); Jones, "Fortifications and Sieges," 174–75; Steven McCotter, "Byzantines, Avars and the Introduction of the Trebuchet" at http://www.deremilitari.org/RESOURCES/ ARTICLES/mccotter1.htm.

31. Chevedden, "Invention of the Counterweight Trebuchet," 71–116.

32. An excellent introduction to naval warfare is Susan Rose, *Medieval Naval Warfare, 1000–1500* (New York: Routledge, 2002). See also Felipe Fernández-Armesto, "Naval Warfare after the Viking Age, c. 1100–1500," in *Medieval Warfare*, ed. Keen, 230–52, esp. 231–32 and John H. Pryor, *Geography, Technology, and War: Studies in the Maritime History of the Mediterranean, 649–1571* (Cambridge: Cambridge University Press, 1992), citation on xvii, and 1–8. See also John B. Hattendorf and Richard W. Unger, eds., *War at Sea in the Middle Ages and the Renaissance* (Woodbridge, U.K.: Boydell Press, 2003) and Unger, *The Ship in the Medieval Economy, 600–1600* (London: Croom Helm, 1980).

33. Nicole, *Medieval Warfare Source Book*, 47 and 87–88.

34. Fernández-Armesto, "Naval Warfare," 234–38.

35. Fernández-Armesto, "Naval Warfare," 238–44. For Greek Fire, see esp. H. R. Ellis Davidson, "The Secret Weapon of Byzantium," *Byzantinische Zeitschrift* 66 (March 1973): 61–74; J. Haldon and M. Byrne, "A Possible Solution to the Problem of Greek Fire," *Byzantinische Zeitschrift* 70 (April 1977): 91–99; Alex Roland, "Secrecy, Technology, and War: Greek Fire and the Defense of Byzantium," *Technology and Culture* 33 (October 1992): 655–79.

36. For the Byzantine navy in the tenth and early eleventh centuries, see John H. Pryor, "Byzantium and the Sea: Byzantine Fleets and the History of the Empire in the Age of the Macedonian Emperors, c. 900–1025 C.E." in *War at Sea,* ed. Hattendorf and Unger, 83–104. For a succinct discussion of the Crusades and their complex historiography, see Jonathan Riley-Smith, "The Crusading Movement and Historians," in *The Oxford History of the Crusades*, ed. Riley-Smith (Oxford: Oxford University Press, 1999), 1–34.

37. John France, *Victory in the East: A Military History of the First Crusade* (Cambridge: Cambridge University Press, 1994), citation on 367. See also Angeliki E. Laiou and Roy Parviz Mottahedeh, ed., *The Crusades from the Perspective of Byzantium and the Muslim World* (Washington, D.C.: Dumbarton Oaks, 2001) and Paul Magadalino, *The Byzantine Background to the First Crusade* (Toronto: Canadian Institute of Balkan Studies, 1996), also available at http://www.deremilitari.org/RESOURCES/ARTICLES/magdalino.htm; R. C. Smail, *Crusading Warfare, 1097–1190*, 2d ed., with a bibliographical introduction by Christopher Marshall (Cambridge: Cambridge University Press, 1995).

38. Malcolm Barber, *The New Knighthood: A History of the Order of the Temple* (Cambridge: Cambridge University Press, 1994); Alan Forey, *The Military Orders from the Twelfth to the Early Fourteenth Centuries* (Toronto: University of Toronto Press, 1992); and, for a concise summary, Forey, "The Military Orders, 1120–1312," in *Oxford History of the Crusades*, ed. Riley-

Smith, 176–210, esp. 182–84. See also Hugh Kennedy, *Crusader Castles* (Cambridge: Cambridge University Press, 1994).

39. Simon Lloyd, "Crusading Movement, 1096–1274," in *Oxford History of the Crusades*, ed. Riley-Smith, 35–67, esp. 59–65. For Islamic reactions to the Crusades, see Carole Hillenbrand, *The Crusades: Islamic Perspectives* (New York: Routledge, 1999).

40. Robert Irwin, "Islam and the Crusades, 1096–1699," in *Oxford History of the Crusades*, ed. Riley-Smith, 211–57, esp. 211–30, does a fine job of explaining the complexity of the situation.

41. Irwin, "Islam and the Crusades," 230–57.

42. Irwin, "Islam and the Crusades," 230–57; see also Reuven Amitai-Preiss, *Mongols and Mamluks: The Mamluk-Ilkhanid War, 1260–1261* (Cambridge: Cambridge University Press, 1995).

CHAPTER 5

1. John L. Langdon, "Transportation, Inland (European)," in *Travel, Trade, and Exploration in the Middle Ages: An Encyclopedia*, ed. John Block Friedman and Kristen Mossler Figg (New York: Garland, 2000), 607–13.

2. Langdon, "Transportation," 609; Paul Hindle, *Medieval Roads and Tracks*, 3d ed. (Buckinghamshire: Shire Publications, 1998); Albert C. Leighton, *Transport and Communication in Early Medieval Europe, A.D. 500–1100* (New York: Barnes and Noble, 1972).

3. Langdon, "Transportation," 609.

4. Langdon, "Transportation," 609; John L. Langdon, *Horses, Oxen and Technological Innovation* (Cambridge: Cambridge University Press, 1986), esp. 114–17 and 142–244; Leighton, *Transport*, 81–90 and 117–22.

5. Langdon, "Transportation," 609; Leighton, *Transport*, 58–59.

6. Leighton, *Transport*, 63–69 and 101–07.

7. Marjorie Nice Boyer, *Medieval French Bridges: A History* (Cambridge, Mass.: Medieval Academy of America, 1976), 8–10, 73–87, and 143–53, citation on 77–78.

8. Donald R. Hill, *Islamic Science and Engineering* (Edinburgh: Edinburgh University Press, 1993), 149–58.

9. Bulliet, *Camel and the Wheel*, esp. 57–140 and 216–36, citation on 217.

10. Daniel E. Schafer, "Caravans," in *Travel, Trade, and Exploration*, ed. Friedman and Figg, 94–96.

11. Schafer, "Caravans."

12. Unger, *Ship in the Medieval Economy*, 21–32, citations on 21 and 25.

13. Jan Bill, "Ship Construction Tools and Techniques," in *Cogs, Caravels and Galleons: The Sailing Ship, 1000–1650*, ed. Robert Gardiner and Richard W. Unger (Annapolis, Md.: Naval Institute Press, 1994), 151–59; Ian Friel, *The Good Ship: Ships, Shipbuilding and Technology in England, 1200–1520* (Baltimore, Md.: Johns Hopkins University Press, 1995), 39–67.

14. Unger, *Ship in the Medieval Economy*, 36–38; and, for a succinct summary, Richard W. Unger, "Ships and Shipbuilding," in *Trade, Travel and Exploration*, ed. Block and Figg, 553–58.

15. See Unger, *Ship in the Medieval Economy*, 39–50, for a detailed discussion of early Byzantine ships; see also Unger, "Ships and Shipbuilding," 554.

16. George F. Hourani, *Arab Seafaring in the Indian Ocean in Ancient and Early Medieval Times*, rev. and expanded by John Carswell (Princeton, N.J.: Princeton University Press, 1995); G. R. Tibbetts, *Arab Navigation in the Indian Ocean before the Coming of the Portuguese being a Translation of Kitāb al-Fawā-id fī usūl al-bahr wa'l-qawā'id of Ahmad b. Mājid al-Najdī* (London: Royal Asiatic Society of Great Britain and Ireland, 1971); S. Maqbul Ahmad, "Djughrafiya, Geography," in *Encyclopaedia of Islam*, ed. Bearman et al., 2:575–87; S. Soucek et al., "Milaha, Navigation, seamanship; seafaring" in *Encyclopaedia of Islam*, ed. Bearman et al., 7:40–53; H. Kindermann et al., "Safina [ship]," in *Encyclopaedia of Islam*, ed. Bearman et al., 8:808–11.

17. Martin Malcolm Elbl, "Hulk" and John E. Dotson, "Cog," in *Trade, Travel and Exploration*, ed. Friedman and Figg, 263–64 and 553–58, respectively; Detlev Ellmers, "The Cog as Cargo Carrier" and Timothy J. Runyon, "The Cog as Warship," in *Cogs, Caravels and Galleons*, ed. Gardiner and Unger, 29–46 and 47–58, respectively; Friel, *Good Ship*; Gillian Hutchinson, *Medieval Ships and Shipping* (Rutherford, Pa.: Fairleigh Dickinson University Press, 1994), esp. 10–15 and 4–46; Archibald R. Lewis and Timothy J. Runyan, *European Naval and Maritime History, 300–1500* (Bloomington: Indiana University Press, 1985), xii; Unger, "Ships and Shipbuilding," 554; Unger, *Ship in the Medieval Economy*, 55–62.

18. Owain T. P. Roberts, "Descendants of Viking Boats," in *Cogs, Caravels and Galleons*, ed. Gardiner and Unger, 11–28; Unger, "Ships and Shipbuilding," 554; Unger, *Ship in the Medieval Economy*, 81–95.

19. John H. Pryor, "The Mediterranean Round Ship," in *Cogs, Caravels and Galleons*, ed. Gardiner and Unger, 119–59.

20. For an introduction to shipping that includes consideration of both military and commercial uses, see Lewis and Runyan, *European Naval and Maritime History*. For medieval commercial exchange between east and west, see David Abulafia, "The Role of Trade in Muslim-Christian Contact during the Middle Ages," in *The Arab Influence in Medieval Europe*, ed. Dionisius A. Agius and Richard Hitchcock (Reading, U.K.: Ithaca Press, 1994), 1–24; Thomas T. Allsen, *Commodity and Exchange in the Mongol Empire: A Cultural History of Islamic Textiles* (Cambridge: Cambridge University Press, 1997); Olivia Remie Constable, *Trade and Traders in Muslim Spain: The Commercial Realignment of the Iberian Peninsula, 900–1500* (Cambridge: Cambridge University Press, 1994); Vladimir P. Goss and Christine Verzár Bornstein, eds., *The Meeting of Two Worlds: Cultural Exchange between East and West during the Period of the Crusades* (Kalamazoo: Western Michigan University Press, 1986).

21. John W. Barker, "Byzantine Empire," in *Trade, Travel and Exploration*, ed. Freeman and Figg, 84–87.

22. Nehemia Levtzion, "Muslim Travelers and Trade," in *Trade, Travel and Exploration*, ed. Freeman and Figg, 418–25, esp. 418–19.

23. Levtzion, "Muslim Travelers and Trade," 418–25; Horden and Purcell, *Corrupting Sea*, 154–56; Barbara M. Kreutz, *Before the Normans: Southern Italy in the Ninth and Tenth Centuries* (Philadelphia: University of Pennsylvania Press, 1991), ch. 5, for Amalfi; Lane, *Venice*, 4–54.

24. Lane, *Venice*, 5–6.

25. Lane, *Venice*, 6–7.

26. Lane, *Venice*, 7–8.

27. McCormick, *Origins of the European Economy*; for a summary, see McCormick, "New Light on the 'Dark Ages,'" 17–54.

28. Goitein, *Mediterranean Society*, 1:27–28 and 42–47.

29. Goitein, *Mediterranean Society*, 1:47–59 and 272–352.

30. Horden and Purcell, *Corrupting Sea*, 53–88 and 123–72.

31. Horden and Purcell, *Corrupting Sea*, 151–52.

32. Horden and Purcell, *Corrupting Sea*, 342–400, citations on 359.

33. Bryan Atherton, "Hanse [The Hanseatic League]," in *Trade, Travel, and Exploration*, ed. Friedman and Figg, 246–48. See also Konrad Fritze, Johannes Schildhauer, and Walter Stark, *Die Geschichte der Hanse*, 2d ed. (Berlin: Verlag

das Europäische Buch, 1985); Johannes Schildhauer, *Tha Hansa: Its History and Culture*, trans. Katherine Vasrovitch (Leipzig: Druckerei Fortschritt Erfurt, 1985); Uwe Ziegler, *Die Hanse* (Bern: Scherz Verlag, 1994).

34. Angeliki E. Laiou, with an appendix by Cécile Morrisson, "Byzantine Trade with Christians and Muslims and the Crusades," in *Crusades*, ed. Laiou and Mottahedeh, 157–96.

CHAPTER 6

1. David Diringer, *The Book before Printing: Ancient, Medieval and Oriental* (New York: Dover, 1982), 126–35; Bloom, *Paper before Print*, 20–23; Michelle P. Brown, *Understanding Illuminated Manuscripts: A Guide to Technical Terms* (Malibu, Calif.: J. Paul Getty Museum and the British Library, 1994), 94–95.

2. Bloom, *Paper before Print*, 20–23; Brown, *Understanding Illuminated Manuscripts*, 42 and 94–95.

3. Carlo Bertelli, "The Production and Distribution of Books in Late Antiquity," in *Sixth Century*, ed. Hodges and Bowden, 41–60; Bloom, *Paper before Print*, 20–23; Brown, *Understanding Illuminated Manuscripts*, 42, 94–95, and 107–08; Diringer, *Book before Printing*, 129–40; Colin H. Roberts and T. C. Skeat, *The Birth of the Codex* (Oxford: British Academy and Oxford University Press, 1983).

4. Bloom, *Paper before Print*, 25–29; Brown, *Understanding Illuminated Manuscripts*, 95.

5. Bloom, *Paper before Print*, 29–45, and, for molds, 67–70; Brown, *Understanding Illuminated Manuscripts*, 93–94.

6. Bloom, *Paper before Print*, 47–52 and 133.

7. Bloom, *Paper before Print*, 107; Brown, *Understanding Illuminated Manuscripts*, 57 and 73; Sherwood Taylor and Charles Singer, "Pre-scientific Industrial Chemistry," in *A History of Technology*, vol. 2, *The Mediterranean Civilizations and the Middle Ages, c. 700 B.C. to c. A.D. 1500*, ed. Singer et al. (New York: Oxford University Press, 1956), 359–60.

8. Bloom, *Paper before Print*, 204–06.

9. Bloom, *Paper before Print*, 206–13.

10. The traditional view can be found in Walter J. Ong, *Orality and Literacy: The Technologizing of the Word* (London: Routlege, 2002) and in Jack Goody, *The Domestication of the Savage Mind* (Cambridge: Cambridge University Press, 1977). See also Goody, *The Interface between the Written and the Oral* (Cambridge: Cambridge University Press, 1987). A critic of these views was Brian V. Street, *Literacy in Theory and Practice* (Cambridge: Cambridge

University Press, 1984). For a more contextual approach, see esp. M. T. Clanchy, *From Memory to Written Record: England, 1066–1307*, 2d ed. (Oxford: Blackwell, 1993), 7–16; Graff, *Legacies of Literacy*, esp. 34–74; Rosamond McKitterick, ed., introduction to *The Uses of Literacy in Early Mediaeval Europe* (Cambridge: Cambridge University Press, 1990), 1–10.

11. Clanchy, *From Memory to Written Record*, 1–21; McKitterick, introduction to *Uses of Literacy*, 1–10; Brian Stock, *The Implications of Literacy: Written Language and Models of Interpretation in the Eleventh and Twelfth Centuries* (Princeton, N.J.: Princeton University Press, 1983).

12. Margaret Mullet, "Writing in Early Mediaeval Byzantium," in *Uses of Literacy in Early Mediaeval Europe*, ed. McKitterick, 156–85.

13. Bloom, *Paper before Print*, 94–97.

14. Wheeler M. Thackston, "The Role of Calligraphy," in *The Mosque*, ed. Frishman and Khan, 42–53, citations on 44 and 45.

15. Graff, *Legacies of Literacy*, 33–52, provides an overview. For studies on the functions of literacy in different locales, see *Uses of Literacy*, ed. McKitterick; McKitterick, "Eighth-Century Foundations," Michel Banniard, "Language and Communication in Carolingian Europe," and David Ganz, "Book Production in the Carolingian Empire and the Spread of the Caroline Minuscule," in *New Cambridge Medieval History*, ed. McKitterick, 2:681–94, 695–708, and 786–808, respectively. See also McKitterick, *The Carolingians and the Written Word* (Cambridge: Cambridge University Press, 1989) and "Carolingian Book Production: Some Problems," in *Books, Scribes and Learning in the Frankish Kingdoms, 6th–9th Centuries*, ed. McKitterick (Aldershot: Variorum, Ashgate, 1994), XII.

16. See Graff, *Legacies of Literacy*, 53–74; Clanchy, *From Memory to Written Record*.

17. Clanchy, *From Memory to Written Record*, 185–96 and 328–34, citation on 334.

18. Alice-Mary Talbot and Ernst Gamillscheg, "Book," in *Oxford Dictionary of Byzantium*, ed. Kazhdan et al., 1:305.

19. Brown, *Understanding Illuminated Manuscripts*, 22 and 98–99; Michele P. Brown, *The British Library Guide to Writing and Scripts: History and Techniques* (Toronto: University of Toronto Press, 1998), 60–61; Christopher de Hamel, *The British Library Guide to Manuscript Illumination: History and Techniques* (Toronto: University of Toronto Press, 2001), esp. 39–81; Robert S. Nelson, "Book Illustration and Illumination," *Oxford Dictionary of Byzantium*, ed. Kazhdan et al., 1:306–08.

20. Rowena Loverance, *Byzantium* (Cambridge, Mass.: Harvard University Press, 1988), 40–41 and Kurt Weitzmann et al., *The Place of Book Illumination in Byzantine Art* (Princeton, N.J.: Art Museum, Princeton University, 1975).

21. Bloom and Blair, *Islamic Arts*, 58–78; Bloom, *Paper before Print*, 99–101; J. Sourdel-Thomine, "Khat (A) Writing," in *Encyclopaedia of Islam*, ed. Bearman et al., 4:1113–22. For calligraphy in mosques, see Thackston, "Role of Calligraphy."

22. Bloom and Blair, *Islamic Arts*, 193–94; see also Johannes Pedersen, *The Arabic Book*, ed. Robert Hillenbrand, trans. Geoffrey French (Princeton, N.J.: Princeton University Press, 1984).

23. Bloom and Blair, *Islamic Arts*, 193–97; Bloom, *Paper before Print*, 92.

24. Bloom, *Paper before Print*, 106–13; see also Sabra, "Appropriation and Subsequent Naturalization," 3–27; Gutas, *Greek Thought, Arabic Culture*.

25. Bloom, *Paper before Print*, 113–23.

26. Brown, *British Library Guide to Writing and Scripts*, 72–78; Brown, *Understanding Illuminated Manuscripts*, 97.

27. Clanchy, *From Memory to Written Record*, 118–25.

28. Bloom, *Paper before Print*, 111–13; Gulnar Bosch, John Carswell, and Guy Petherbridge, *Islamic Bindings and Bookmaking: A Catalogue of an Exhibition, The Oriental Institute, The University of Chicago, May 18–August 18, 1981* (Chicago: Oriental Institute Museum, University of Chicago, 1981); Clanchy, *From Memory to Written Record*, 117; de Hamel, *British Library Guide to Manuscript Illumination*, esp. 39–81, 88; Duncan Haldane, *Islamic Book Bindings in the Victoria and Albert Museum* (London: World of Islam Festival Trust in association with Victoria and Albert Museum, 1983); Philippa J. M. Marks, *The British Library Guide to Bookbinding: History and Techniques* (London: The British Library, 1998), 9 and 29–84.

29. See Gutas, *Greek Thought, Arabic Culture*; and, for a brief discussion, David C. Lindberg, *The Beginnings of Western Science: The European Scientific Tradition in Philosophical, Religious, and Institutional Context, 600 B.C. to A.D. 1450* (Chicago: University of Chicago Press, 1992), 161–82. For the case of astronomy, see George Saliba, *A History of Arabic Astronomy: Planetary Theories during the Golden Age of Islam* (New York: New York University Press, 1994), 51–65.

30. A summary can be found in Edward Grant, *The Foundations of Modern Science in the Middle Ages: Their Religious, Institutional, and Intellectual Contexts* (Cambridge: Cambridge University Press, 1996), 22–53. See also Charles Homer Haskins, *The Renaissance of the Twelfth Century* (New York: World Publishing Co., 1965), 278–303.

CONCLUSION

1. Horden and Purcell, *Corrupting Sea*, 372–75 and 612–15 for amphorae and 612–14 for underwater archaeology; McCormick, *Origins of the European Economy*.

2. Francesca Bray, Technology and Gender: Fabrics of Power in Late Imperial China (Berkeley and Los Angeles: University of California Press, 1997), 1–47.

3. Flood, *Great Mosque of Damascus*, 114–38.

BIBLIOGRAPHIC ESSAY

A comprehensive bibliography on the history of medieval technology would run to hundreds of pages. In addition to general studies, it would include numerous local studies published in the periodicals of specialists in archaeology and history, written in many languages. This essay instead comprises an introductory bibliography, made up mostly but not entirely of English-language works. It provides an introduction to the field as a whole and a gateway into the specialist literature. Although it does not recapitulate every reference in the footnotes, it contains many classic studies as well as some of the best new studies—a place to start in a field of study that is historically rich and presently lively.

For the entire medieval period, a still-essential reference is Charles Singer et al., *A History of Technology*, vol. 2: *The Mediterranean Civilizations and the Middle Ages, c. 700 B.C. to c. A.D. 1500* (New York: Oxford University Press, 1956). Also still useful is M. M. Postan et al., eds., *Cambridge Economic History of Europe*, vol. 1: *Agrarian Life of the Middle Ages*, ed. Postan, and vol. 2: *Trade and Industry in the Middle Ages*, ed. Postan and Edward Miller assisted by Cynthia Postan, 2d ed. (Cambridge: Cambridge University Press, 1966 and 1987). Joseph Strayer, ed., *Dictionary of the Middle Ages*, 13 vols. (New York: Charles Scribner's Sons, 1982-89), contains useful articles on technological subjects, although by now somewhat dated, from agriculture to various crafts. A useful reference is the more recent encyclopedia: Jane Turner, ed., *The Dictionary of Art*, 34 vols. (New York: Grove, 1996), which includes excellent technical articles on subjects related to art and architecture. F.A.C. Mantello and A.G. Rigg, *Medieval Latin: An Introduction and Bibliographical Guide* (Washington, D.C.: Catholic University of America Press, 1996), contains articles on Latin terminology for medieval crafts, industries, agriculture, mining, and other material practices. A useful medieval website which includes many primary sources is http://www.the-orb.net. Essential references for Byzantium and Arabic technologies are Alexander P. Kazhdan et al., eds., *The Oxford Dictionary of Byzantium*, 3 vols. (Oxford: Oxford University Press, 1991); and the P. J. Bearman et al., eds. *Encyclopaedia of Islam*, new ed.,11 vols. (Leiden: Brill, 1978-2001), both of which contain excellent articles on technological subjects.

For a discussion of the Pirenne thesis and the relevance of medieval archaeology to its evaluation, see Richard Hodges and David Whitehouse, *Mohammed, Charlemagne and the Origins of Europe: Archaeology and the Pirenne Thesis* (Ithaca, N.Y.: Cornell University Press, 1983); and Richard Hodges and William Bowden, eds., *The Sixth Century: Production, Distribution and Demand* (Leiden: Brill, 1998). Two books on archaeology especially useful for historians are Kevin Greene, *The Archaeology of the Roman Economy* (Berkeley and Los Angeles: University of California Press, 1990); and Klavs Randsborg, *The First Millennium A.D. in Europe and the Mediterranean: An Archaeological Essay* (Cambridge: Cambridge University Press, 1991). An important study with particular relevance to the Pirenne thesis is Michael McCormick, *Origins of the European Economy: Communications and Commerce, A.D. 300-900* (Cambridge: Cambridge University Press, 2001).

For the Byzantine Empire, see especially Warren T. Treadgold, *A History of the Byzantine State and Society* (Stanford, Calif.: Stanford University Press, 1997). Two excellent introductory surveys are Robert Browning, *The Byzantine Empire*, rev. ed. (Washington, D.C.: Catholic University Press, 1992); and Cyril Mango, *Byzantium: The Empire of the New Rome* (New York: Charles Scribner's Sons, 1980). For the middle and later periods, see Mark Whittow, *The Making of Byzantium, 600-1025* (Berkeley and Los Angeles: University of California Press, 1996). Readable essays centered on types of individuals (peasants, the poor, entrepreneurs) can be found in Guglielmo Cavallo, ed., *The Byzantines*, trans. Thomas Dunlap et al. (Chicago: University of Chicago Press, 1997). For recent scholarship, see Cyril Mango, ed., *The Oxford History of Byzantium* (Oxford: Oxford University Press, 2002). Russian scholars who saw in Byzantine villages and agricultural systems a model for their own agricultural reforms began the modern study of Byzantine agriculture in the early twentieth century. Their work, written in Russian and never translated, is relatively unknown. However, Russian scholars such as Georg Ostrogorsky continued this earlier work. Representative is Ostrogorsky's "Agrarian Conditions in the Byzantine Empire in the Middle Ages," in Postan, ed., *Cambridge Economic History*, vol. 1: *Agrarian Life*, 205-34. Earlier work has been criticized for its inappropriate focus on "feudalism," a model more appropriate for the west than for Byzantium. Significant work on Byzantine agriculture includes Paul Lemerle, *The Agrarian History of Byzantium from the Origins to the Twelfth Century: The Sources and Problems* (Galway, Ireland: Galway University Press, 1979); Michel Kaplan, *Les Hommes et la Terre à Byzance du VIe au XIe Siècle* (Paris: Publications de la Sorbonne, 1992); and Angeliki E. Laiou-Thomadakis, *Peasant Society in the Late Byzantine Empire: A Social and Demographic Study* (Princeton, N.J.: Princeton University Press, 1977). A careful study of agricultural tools with attention to both extant objects and visual depictions is Anthony Bryer, "Byzantine Agricultural Implements: The Evidence of Medieval Illustrations of Hesiod's *Works and Days*," *The Annual of the British School at Athens* 81 (1986): 45-80. Any student of early medieval agricultural implements will also want to study K. D. White's *Agricultural Implements of the Roman World* (Cambridge: Cambridge University Press, 1967).

While discussions of *Hagia Sophia* in Constantinople abound, attention to the building's technical characteristics are much less common. A cogent discussion of the dome with reference to ancient domes can be found in Robert Mark, *Light, Wind, and Structure: The Mystery of the Master Builders* (Cambridge, Mass.: MIT Press, 1990), 73-89. Detailed technical discussions which require some technical or architectural-history background for full comprehension are Robert Mark and Ahmet Ş. Çakmak, eds., *Hagia Sophia from the Age of Justinian to the Present* (Cambridge: Cambridge University Press, 1992); and Rowland J. Mainstone, *Hagia Sophia: Architecture, Structure and Liturgy of Justinian's Great Church* (New York: Thames and Hudson, 1997). For a later period, a study centered on the techniques of the masons, including detailed discussion of many middle Byzantine buildings is Robert Ousterhout's *Master Builders of Byzantium* (Princeton, N.J.: Princeton University Press, 1999). Besim S. Hakim, "Julian of Ascalon's Treatise of Construction and Design Rules from Sixth-Century Palestine," *Journal of the Society of Architectural Historians* 60 (March 2001): 4-25, provides a fascinating glimpse of a medieval city through an important primary source.

The classic study of the Byzantine silk industry is Robert Sabatino Lopez, "Silk Industry in the Byzantine Empire," *Speculum* 20 (January 1945): 1-42. Recent scholarship begins with the work of Anna Muthesius, *Byzantine Silk Weaving, A.D. 400 to A.D. 1200* (Vienna: Verlag Fassbaender, 1997); and Muthesius, *Studies in Byzantine and Islamic Silk Weaving* (London: Pindar Press, 1995). Muthesius's exemplary methodology is fundamentally interdisciplinary and includes study of both documentary and archaeological sources; detailed knowledge of extant pieces of silk; attention to DNA findings with regard to silkworms (showing that all silkworms did not come from China); study of traditional weaving in neighboring cultures such as China and India; and experimental weaving which attempts to construct traditional looms and to replicate extant Byzantine silk.

Other Byzantine technologies that have received welcome attention include the archaeological finds of oil presses and mills in Syria, published by Olivier Callot, "Huileries antique de Syrie du Nord," *Bibliothèque archéologique et historique* 118 (1984): 1-128, which includes numerous drawings depicting the sites and machines discovered. The study of Byzantine ivories by Anthony Cutler, *The Hand of the Master: Craftsmanship, Ivory, and Society in Byzantium (9th-11th Centuries)* (Princeton, N.J.: Princeton University Press, 1994), shows that detailed attention to the objects themselves can reveal a wealth of information about craft processes and techniques.

Primary sources for Byzantine history include a rich tradition of military writings, many of which have been made widely available in translation. See, especially, George T. Dennis, trans., *Maurice's Strategikon: Handbook of Byzantine Military Strategy* (Philadelphia: University of Pennsylvania Press, 1984); Dennis, *Three Byzantine Military Treatises* (Washington, D.C.: Dumbarton Oaks, 1985); Eric McGeer, *Sowing the Dragon's Teeth: Byzantine Warfare in the Tenth Century* (Washington, D.C.: Dumbarton Oaks, 1995); and Denis F. Sullivan, *Siegecraft: Two Tenth-Century Instructional Manuals by "Heron of Byzantium"* (Washington, D.C.: Dumbarton Oaks, 2000).

Comprehensive accounts of Arab society and the Islamic conquests can be found in Fred McGraw Donner, *The Early Islamic Conquests* (Princeton, N.J.: Princeton University Press, 1981); and Ira. M. Lapidus, *A History of Islamic Societies*, 2d ed. (Cambridge: Cambridge University Press, 2002). The articles (many cited in the notes to this booklet) in A. L. Udovitch, ed., *The Islamic Middle East, 700-1900* (Princeton, N.J.: Darwin Press, 1981), provide excellent introductions to issues of land tenure, agriculture, and irrigation in a variety of Islamic territories from the Sasanian Empire to al-Andalus. A classic study is

Richard W. Bulliet, *The Camel and the Wheel* (New York: Columbia University Press, Morningside Edition, 1990). A general introduction which includes technological topics is Susan L. Douglass, *World Eras*, vol. 2: *Rise and Spread of Islam, 622-1500* (Detroit, Mich.: Gale, 2002). Studies based on the archaeological excavation of particular cities reveal much of interest to historians of technology; see, for example, Chase F. Robinson, *A Medieval Islamic City Reconsidered: An Interdisciplinary Approach to Samarra* (Oxford: Oxford University Press, 2001). Almad Y. al-Hassan and Donald R. Hill, *Islamic Technology: An Illustrated History* (Cambridge: Cambridge University Press, and Paris: UNESCO, 1986), provides a basic introduction that cries out for a more comprehensive and contextually oriented sequel.

For Islamic Spain or al-Andalus with special reference to agriculture and irrigation technologies, the work of Thomas F. Glick is fundamental. See, especially, Glick, *Islamic and Christian Spain in the Early Middle Ages* (Princeton, N.J.: Princeton University Press, 1979); Glick, *Irrigation and Society in Medieval Valencia* (Cambridge, Mass.: Belknap Press of Harvard University, 1970); Glick, *Irrigation and Hydraulic Technology: Medieval Spain and its Legacy* (Aldershot: Variorum, Ashgate, 1996); and, in a broader vein, Glick, *From Muslim Fortress to Christian Castle: Social and Cultural Change in Medieval Spain* (Manchester, U.K.: Manchester University Press, 1995). For the "green revolution" of the Islamic world, see Andrew M. Watson, *Agricultural Innovation in the Early Islamic World: The Diffusion of Crops and Farming Techniques, 700-1100* (Cambridge: Cambridge University Press, 1983); and see Thorkild Schiøler, *Roman and Islamic Water-Lifting Wheels* (Odense: Odense University Press, 1973).

Although the literature on Islamic architecture and arts is relatively large, much of it is focused on aesthetic concerns rather than technical processes. For Islamic architecture and building techniques, see George Michell, ed., *Architecture of the Islamic World: Its History and Meaning* (London: Thames and Hudson, 1978). An exemplary article which provides welcome technical details is Ronald Lewcock, "Materials and Techniques," in Michell, ed., *Architecture of the Islamic World*, 129-143. See also K. A. C. Cresswell, *A Short Account of Early Muslim Architecture*, rev. and supplemented by James W. Allan (Aldershot: Scolar Press, 1989); Martin Frishman and Hasan-Uddin Khan, eds., *The Mosque: History, Architectural Development and Regional Diversity* (London: Thames and Hudson, 1994); and Finnbarr Barry Flood, *The Great Mosque of Damascus: Studies on the Makings of an Umayyad Visual Culture* (Leiden: Brill, 2001). Both architecture and the arts are treated in Robert Hillenbrand, *Islamic Art and Architecture* (London: Thames and Hudson, 1999); Jonathan Bloom and Sheila Blair, *Islamic Arts* (London: Phaidon Press, 1997); and Richard Ettinghausen and Oleg Grabar, *The Art and Architecture of Islam, 650-1250* (New Haven, Conn.: Yale University Press, 1994). The transformation of the ancient city into the Islamic is treated in an important article by Hugh Kennedy, "From *Polis* to *Madina*: Urban Change in Late Antique and Early Islamic Syria," *Past and Present* 106 (February 1985): 3-27.

For Islamic textiles, in addition to the relevant chapters in Bloom and Blair, *Islamic Arts*, see especially Thomas T. Allsen, *Commodity and Exchange in the Mongol Empire: A Cultural History of Textiles* (Cambridge: Cambridge University Press, 1997); Robert B. Serjeant, *Islamic Textiles* (Beirut: Librairie du Liban 1972), a classic investigation of the documentary sources; Patricia L. Baker, *Islamic Textiles* (London: British Museum Press, 1995); Kjeld von Folsach and Anne-Marie Keblow Bernsted, *Woven Treasures: Textiles from the World of Islam*, trans. Martha Gaber Abrahamsen (Copenhagen: The David Collection, 1993); and Muthesius, *Studies in Byzantine and Islamic Silk Weaving*. A fundamental source for knowledge about work, travel, trade, and daily life are the thousands of Geniza documents discovered in a storage area of a synagogue in the late nineteenth century; the classic work on the subject by a scholar who spent his lifetime studying them is S. D. Goitein, *A Mediterranean Society: The Jewish Communities of the Arab World as Portrayed in the Documents of the Cairo Geniza*, 6 vols. (Berkeley and Los Angeles: University of California Press, 1967-1993). An important study of work in the medieval Islamic world is Maya Shatzmiller, *Labour in the Medieval Islamic World* (Leiden: E.J. Brill, 1994). For Islamic tiles, see Venetia Porter, *Islamic Tiles* (New York: Interlink Books, 1995); and for metalwork, Rachel Ward, *Islamic Metalwork* (New York: Thames and Hudson, 1993).

For Islamic engineering and mechanical arts, two important primary sources are available in English translation: Donald R. Hill, ed. and trans., *The Book of Ingenious Devices by the Banu (sons of) Musa bin Shakir* (Dordrecht: D. Reidel, 1979); and Ibn al-Razzaz al-Jazari, *The Book of Knowledge of Ingenious Mechanical Devices*, trans. Donald R. Hill (Dordrecht: Reidel, 1974). See also Hill, *Islamic Science and Engineering* (Edinburgh: Edinburgh University Press, 1993); and Hill, *Studies in Medieval Islamic Technology: From Philo to al-Jazari, from Alexandria to Diyar Bakr*, ed. David A. King (Aldershot: Ashgate, 1998). For Islamic instruments, see especially David A. King, *Islamic Astronomical Instruments* (London: Variorum Reprints, 1987); King and George Saliba, eds., *From Deferent to Equant: A Volume of Studies in the History of Science in the Ancient and Medieval Near East in Honor of E. S. Kennedy* (New York: New York Academy of Sciences, 1987); and Sharon Gibbs with Saliba, *Planispheric Astrolabes from the National Museum of American History* (Washington, D.C.: Smithsonian Institution Press, 1984).

For western Europe, see Rosamond McKitterick, ed., *The New Cambridge Medieval History*, vol. 2: *c. 700-c. 900* (Cambridge: Cambridge University Press, 1995); and Timothy Reuter, ed., *The New Cambridge Medieval History*, vol. 3: *c. 900-c. 1024* (Cambridge: Cambridge University Press, 1999). A more basic introduction is Jeremiah Hackett, ed., *World Eras*, vol. 4; *Medieval Europe, 814-1350* (Detroit: Gale Group, 2002), and for an excellent one-volume synthesis, Robert Bartlett, *The Making of Europe: Conquest, Colonization and Cultural Change, 950-1350* (London: Allen Lane, Penguin Press, 1993). For a popular and competent account focused on technology, see Frances Gies and Joseph

Gies, *Cathedral, Forge, and Waterwheel: Technology and Invention in the Middle Ages* (New York: HarperCollins, 1995). Studies which pay considerable attention to labor and technology include Christopher Dyer, *Making a Living in the Middle Ages: The People of Britain, 850-1520* (New Haven, Conn.: Yale University Press, 2002); Hans-Werner Goetz, *Life in the Middle Ages from the Seventh to the Thirteenth Century*, trans. Albert Wimmer, ed. Steven Rowan (Notre Dame, Ind.: University of Notre Dame Press, 1993); and Adriaan Verhulst, *The Carolingian Economy* (Cambridge: Cambridge University Press, 2002). For broad-ranging studies of water and water technologies, see Roberta J. Magnusson, *Water Technology in the Middle Ages* (Baltimore, Md.: Johns Hopkins University Press, 2001); and Paolo Squatriti, *Water and Society in Early Medieval Italy, AD 400-1000* (Cambridge: Cambridge University Press, 1998).

The historiography of technology including agriculture in the medieval west includes classic studies which spawned further research as well as major critiques and revisions. These works include Marc Bloch, *French Rural History: An Essay on its Basic Characteristics*, trans. Janet Sondheimer (London: Routledge & Kegan Paul, 1966); and Marc Bloch, *Land and Work in Mediaeval Europe: Selected Papers by Marc Bloch*, trans. J.E. Anderson (New York: Harper Torchbooks, 1967). Abbot Payson Usher, *A History of Mechanical Inventions*, rev. ed. (Cambridge, Mass.: Harvard University Press, 1962), includes an extensive discussion of "empirical economic history" as well as detailed accounts of particular technologies that include material on the medieval centuries, such as waterwheels and windmills, water clocks, and the machinery of the textile industries. For Lynn White Jr.'s work, see first the classic *Medieval Technology and Social Change* (London: Oxford University Press, 1962); and also the useful collection of some of his later essays, *Medieval Religion and Technology* (Berkeley and Los Angeles: University of California Press, 1986). Another widely cited account is Jean Gimpel, *The Medieval Machine: The Industrial Revolution of the Middle Ages* (Harmondsworth: Penguin Books, 1976).

Mills have been the focus of substantial scholarship. A classic study is Marc Bloch, "The Advent and Triumph of the Watermill," in *Land and Work in Mediaeval Europe,* 136-168. An important perspective for medieval studies is Örjan Wikander, "Water-Mills in Ancient Rome," *Opuscula Romana* 12 (1979): 13-36; and see Wikander, *Handbook of Ancient Water Technology* (Leiden: E. J. Brill, 2000). For England, see Richard Holt, *the Mills of Medieval England* (Oxford: Basil Blackwell, 1988). For northern Italy, see especially two articles by John Muendel in *Technology and Culture*: "The Horizontal Mills of Medieval Pistoia," 15 (January 1974): 194-225, and "The Internal Functions of a 14th-Century Florentine Flour Factory," 32 (July 1991): 498-520. Adam Lucas, *Wind, Water, Work: Milling Technology in the Ancient and Medieval Worlds* (Leiden: E. J. Brill, forthcoming), offers an important revisionist assessment based on a thorough survey of the evidence and literature of medieval milling. A fine collection of articles ranging from building construction to mills to mines is Elizabeth Bradford Smith and Michael Wolfe, eds., *Technology and Resource Use in*

Medieval Europe: Cathedrals, Mills, and Mines (Aldershot: Ashgate, 1997). For agriculture in the west, see the important synthesis of Georges Duby, *Rural Economy and Country Life in the Medieval West*, trans. Cynthia Postan (Columbia, S.C.: University of South Carolina Press, 1968), which contains a useful selection of documents. A collection of very substantial essays is Grenville Astill and John Langdon, eds., *Medieval Farming and Technology: The Impact of Agricultural Change in Northwest Europe* (Leiden: Brill, 1997); and see as well, Del Sweeney, ed., *Agriculture in the Middle Ages: Technology, Practice, and Representation* (Philadelphia: University of Pennsylvania Press, 1995). Substantial recent studies of medieval agriculture and peasant life include Georges Comet, *Le paysan et son outile: Essai d'histoire technique des cereals (France, VIIIe-XVe siècle)* (Rome: École Française de Rome, 1992); Robert Fossier, *Peasant Life in the Medieval West*, trans. Juliet Vale (Oxford: Basil Blackwell, 1988); and Werner Rösener, *Peasants in the Middle Ages*, trans. Alexander Stützer (Urbana, Ill.: University of Illinois Press, 1992). Barbara A. Hanawalt, *The Ties That Bound: Peasant Families in Medieval England* (New York: Oxford University Press, 1986), is an important study especially useful for issues of work and gender. Essential specialized studies include John Langdon, *Horses, Oxen and Technological Innovation: The Use of Draught Animals in English Farming from 1066 to 1500* (Cambridge: Cambridge University Press, 1986). For the Cistercians, see especially Constance Hoffman Berman, *Medieval Agriculture, the Southern French Countryside, and the Early Cistercians: A Study of Forty-three Monasteries*, in *Transactions of the American Philosophical Society*, vol. 76, part 5, 1986; and see Anna Götlind, *The Messengers of Medieval Technology?: Cistercians and Technology in Medieval Scandinavia* (Alingsås: Viktoria Bokförlag and the Department of History, University of Göteborg, Sweden, 1990).

For medieval crafts, an indispensable collection is John Blair and Nigel Ramsay, eds., *English Medieval Industries: Craftsmen, Techniques, Products* (London: Hambledon Press, 1991); and see also D. W. Crossley, ed., *Medieval Industry* (London: Council for British Archaeology, 1981); and see Heather Swanson, *Medieval Artisans: An Urban Class in Late Medieval England* (Oxford: Basil Blackwell, 1989). For medieval towns, including discussion of artisans and crafts, see Edward Miller and John Hatcher, *Medieval England: Towns, Commerce and Crafts, 1086-1348* (London: Longman, 1995); Richard Holt and Gervase Rosser, *The English Medieval Town: A Reader in English Urban History, 1200-1540* (London: Longman, 1990); David Nicholas, *The Growth of the Medieval City: From Late Antiquity to the Early Fourteenth Century* (London: Longman, 1997); and D. M. Palliser, ed., *The Cambridge Urban History of Britain*, vol. 1: *600-1540* (Cambridge: Cambridge University Press, 2000). Especially for information concerning urban archaeology, see Richard Hodges and Brian Hobley, *The Rebirth of Towns in the West, AD 700-1050* (London: Council for British Archaeology, 1988). For textiles see David T. Jenkins, ed., *The Cambridge History of Western Textiles*, 2 vols. (New York:

Cambridge University Press, 2003). For textiles in England and the low countries, with particular attention to techniques, see especially John H. Munro, *Textiles, Towns and Trade: Essays in the Economic History of Late-Medieval England and the Low Countries* (Aldershot: Ashgate, Variorum 1994). For cotton cloth production, see Maureen Fennell Mazzaoui, *The Italian Cotton Industry in the Late Middle Ages, 1100-1600* (Cambridge: Cambridge University Press, 1981). For engineering, see Donald R. Hill, *A History of Engineering in Classical and Medieval Times* (London: Routledge, 1996); and for gender and work, Barbara A. Hanawalt, ed., *Women and Work in Preindustrial Europe* (Bloomington, Ind.: Indiana University Press, 1986). For craft guilds, see Steven A. Epstein, *Wage Labor and Guilds in Medieval Europe* (Chapel Hill, N.C.: University of North Carolina Press, 1991).

Architecture and building techniques in the medieval west are treated in the following classic accounts: John Fitchen, *The Construction of Gothic Cathedrals: A Study of Medieval Vault Erection* (Chicago: The University of Chicago Press, 1981); Fitchen, *Building Construction before Mechanization* (Cambridge, Mass.: MIT Press, 1986); and L. F. Salzman, *Building in England Down to 1540: A Documentary History* (Oxford: Clarendon Press, 1992). A study that devotes much attention to actual structures and archaeological evidence is Jean Chapelot and Robert Fossier, *The Village and the House in the Middle Ages*, trans. Henry Cleere (Berkeley and Los Angeles: University of California Press, 1985). For an analysis of large-scale building structures, see especially Robert Mark, *Experiments in Gothic Structure* (Cambridge, Mass.: MIT Press, 1983); and Mark, *Light, Wind, and Structure: The Mystery of the Master Builders* (Cambridge, Mass.: MIT Press, 1990). See also Lynn T. Courtenay, ed., *The Engineering of Medieval Cathedrals* (Aldershot: Ashgate, 1997); Jacques Heyman, *Arches, Vaults and Buttresses: Masonry Structures and their Engineering* (Aldershot: Variorum, Ashgate, 1996); and Nancy Y. Wu, *Ad quadratum: The Practical Application of Geometry in Medieval Architecture* (Aldershot: Ashgate, 2002). For castles, see Charles L. H. Coulson, *Castles in Medieval Society: Fortresses in England, France, and Ireland in the Central Middle Ages* (Oxford: Oxford University Press, 2003); Hugh Kennedy, *Crusader Castles* (Cambridge: Cambridge University Press, 1994); M. W. Thompson, *The Rise of the Castle* (Cambridge: Cambridge University Press, 1991); and Philip Warner, *The Medieval Castle: Life in a Fortress in Peace and War* (London: Penguin, 2001).

For an introduction to scholarship on the Vikings, see especially Peter Sawyer, ed., *The Oxford Illustrated History of the Vikings* (Oxford: Oxford University Press, 1997); and Paddy Griffith, *The Viking Art of War* (London: Greenhill Books, 1995).

Studies pertaining to the status of work, and of the mechanical arts, and to issues of technology and gender, include Jacques Le Goff, *Time, Work, and Culture in the Middle Ages*, trans. Arthur Goldhammer (Chicago: University of Chicago Press, 1980); David Herlihy, *Opera Mulierbria: Women and Work in*

Medieval Europe (Philadelphia: Temple University Press, 1990); Birgit van den Hoven, *Work in Ancient and Medieval Thought: Ancient Philosophers, Medieval Monks and Theologians and Their Concept of Work, Occupations, and Technology* (Amsterdam: J. C. Gieben, 1996); Pamela O. Long, *Openness, Secrecy, Authorship: Technical Arts and the Culture of Knowledge from Antiquity to the Renaissance* (Baltimore, Md.: Johns Hopkins University Press, 2001); George Ovitt, *The Restoration of Perfection: Labor and Technology in Medieval Culture* (New Brunswick, N.J.: Rutgers University Press, 1987); and Elspeth Whitney, *Paradise Restored: The Mechanical Arts from Antiquity through the Thirteenth Century,* in *Transactions of the American Philosophical Society*, n.s., 80, part 1, 1990.

Medieval military history, including technological aspects, is a large and growing specialty. For a comprehensive bibliography, see Kelly DeVries, *A Cumulative Bibliography of Medieval Military History and Technology* (Leiden: E. J. Brill, 2002). Classic introductions to warfare in the medieval west include Philippe Contamine, *War in the Middle Ages,* trans. Michael Jones (Oxford: Basil Blackwell, 1984); and J. F. Verbruggen, *The Art of Warfare in Western Europe During the Middle Ages from the Eighth Century to 1340,* 2d ed., trans. Sumner Willard and Mrs. R. W. Southern (Woodbridge, Suffolk: Boydell Press, 1997). Recent monographs include Bernard S. Bachrach, *Early Carolingian Warfare: Prelude to Empire* (Philadelphia: University of Pennsylvania Press, 2001); John France, *Western Warfare in the Age of the Crusades, 100-1300* (Ithaca, N.Y.: Cornell University Press, 1999); John Haldon, *Warfare, State and Society in the Byzantine World, 565-1204* (London: University College London Press, 1999); Michael Prestwich, *Armies and Warfare in the Middle Ages: The English Experience* (New Haven, Conn.: Yale University Press, 1996); Christopher Marshall, *Warfare in the Latin East, 1192-1291* (Cambridge: Cambridge University Press, 1992); and see also Warren T. Treadgold, *Byzantium and Its Army, 284-1081* (Stanford, Calif.: Stanford University Press, 1995); and Mark C. Bartusis, *The Late Byzantine Army: Arms and Society, 1204-1453* (Philadelphia: University of Pennsylvania Press, 1992). A useful collection of scholarly essays is Maurice Keen, ed., *Medieval Warfare: A History* (Oxford: Oxford University Press, 1999). For the siege, see Jim Bradbury, *The Medieval Siege* (Woodbridge: Boydell Press, 1992); Ivy A. Corfis and Michael Wolfe, eds., *The Medieval City under Siege* (Woodbridge: Boydell Press, 1995); and Randall Rogers, *Latin Siege Warfare in the Twelfth Century* (Oxford: Clarendon Press, 1992). For military technology, see Claude Blair, *European Armour circa 1066 to circa 1700* (London: B. T. Batsford, 1958); Kelly DeVries, *Medieval Military Technology* (Peterborough, Ontario: Broadview Press, 1992); and David Nicolle, *Medieval Warfare Source Book: Christian Europe and its Neighbors* (London: Brockhampton Press, 1998), which includes extensive pictorial material. For the trebuchet, see especially Paul E. Chevedden, "The Invention of the Counterweight Trebuchet: a Study in Cultural Diffusion," in Mary-Alice Talbot, ed., *Dumbarton Oaks Papers, No.* 54 (Washington, D.C.: Dumbarton Oaks, 2000), 71-116.

For the Crusades, see R. C. Smail, *Crusading Warfare, 1097-1193* (Cambridge: Cambridge University Press, 1995); and also John France, *Victory in the East: A Military History of the First Crusade* (Cambridge: Cambridge University Press, 1994); Paul Magadalino, *The Byzantine Background to the First Crusade* (Toronto: Canadian Institute of Balkan Studies, 1996), also available at http://www.deremilitari.org/RESOURCES/ARTICLES/magdalino.htm; Jonathan Riley Smith, *The Oxford History of the Crusades* (Oxford: Oxford University Press, 1999); Angeliki E. Laiou and Roy Parviz Mottahedeh, eds., *The Crusades from the Perspective of Byzantium and the Muslim World* (Washington, D.C.: Dumbarton Oaks, 2000); and Carole Hillenbrand, *The Crusades: Islamic Perspectives* (New York: Routledge, 1999). For the military orders, see Malcolm Barber, *The New Knighthood: A History of the Order of the Temple* (Cambridge: Cambridge University Press, 1994); and Alan Forey, *The Military Orders From the Twelfth to the Early Fourteenth Centuries* (Toronto: University of Toronto Press, 1992). A useful scholarly website devoted to medieval military history is http://www.deremilitari.org.

Travel, transportation, and commerce are the focus of a recent encyclopedia, John Block Friedman and Kristen Mossler Figg, eds., *Trade, Travel, and Exploration in the Middle Ages: An Encyclopedia* (New York: Garland Publishing, 2000). For extensive and fascinating information about travel and trade, see Goitein, *A Mediterranean Society*, vol. 1: *Economic Foundations*. Bulliet, *The Camel and the Wheel* is essential to any consideration of medieval transportation. A recent study, Peregrine Horden and Nicholas Purcell, *The Corrupting Sea: A Study of Mediterranean History* (Oxford: Blackwell, 2000), develops an important methodological thesis concerning small regions and micro-ecology and has much to say about travel and commerce in the Mediterranean. McCormick, *Origins of the European Economy*, emphasizes the vitality of Carolingian commerce as it also utilizes new methodologies and provides much new data. For the role of Venice, Frederic C. Lane's *Venice: A Maritime Republic* (Baltimore, Md.: Johns Hopkins University Press, 1973), is a classic study and still the place to start. Somewhat outdated but still useful is Albert C. Leighton, *Transport and Communication in Early Medieval Europe, AD 500–1100* (New York: Barnes and Noble, 1972); and see also Marjorie Nice Boyer, *Medieval French Bridges: A History* (Cambridge, Mass.: Mediaeval Academy of America, 1976); and Paul Hindle, *Medieval Roads and Tracks*, 3rd ed. (Buckinghamshipre, U.K.: Shire Publications, 1998).

Medieval ships are the focus of numerous studies, increasingly enhanced by underwater archaeological discoveries of wrecks. See especially Richard W. Unger, *The Ship in the Medieval Economy, 600–1600* (London: Croom Helm, 1980), and Robert Gardiner, ed., *Cogs, Caravels and Galleons: The Sailing Ship, 1000-1650* (Annapolis: Naval Institute Press, 1994). For English ships and shipping, see Ian Friel, *The Good Ship: Ships, Shipbuilding and Technology in England, 1200–1520* (Baltimore, Md.: Johns Hopkins University Press, 1995); and Gillian Hutchinson, *Medieval Ships and Shipping* (Rutherford, Penn.: Fairleigh Dickinson University Press, 1994). An important study of pictorial evidence is Richard W. Unger, *The Art of Medieval Technology: Images of Noah the Shipbuilder* (New Brunswick, N.J.: Rutgers University Press, 1991). For naval warfare, see especially John B. Hattendorf and Richard W. Unger, *War at Sea in the Middle Ages and the Renaissance* (Woodbridge, U.K.: Boydell Press, 2003); and John Haywood, *Dark Age Naval Power: A Re-Assessment of Frankish and Anglo-Saxon Seafaring Activity* (New York: Routledge, 1991). For Arab seafaring on the Indian Ocean, essential studies include George F. Hourani, *Arab Seafaring in the Indian Ocean in Ancient and Early Medieval Times*, rev. and expanded by John Carswell (Princeton, N.J.: Princeton University Press, 1995); and G. B. Tibbetts, *Arab Navigation in the Indian Ocean before the Coming of the Portuguese being a Translation of Kitāb al-Fawā'id fī usūl al-bahr wa'l-qawā'id of Ahmad b. Mājid al-Najdī* (London: The Royal Asiatic Society of Great Britain and Ireland, 1971).

The topics of writing, reading, and literacy are the focus of a massive literature. For an overview, see Harvey J. Graff, *The Legacies of Literacy: Continuities and Contradictions in Western Culture and Society* (Bloomington, Ind.: Indiana University Press, 1987). M. T. Clanchy's *From Memory to Written Record: England 1066-1307*, 2d ed. (Oxford: Blackwell, 1993), is a classic and influential study with implications that extend beyond the geographical boundaries mentioned in the title. See also the important work of Rosamond McKitterick, *The Carolingians and the Written Word* (Cambridge: Cambridge University Press, 1989); McKitterick, *Books, Scribes and Learning in the Frankish Kingdoms, 6th-9th Centuries* (Aldershot: Ashgate, Variorum, 1994); and McKitterick, ed., *The Uses of Literacy in Early Mediaeval Europe* (Cambridge: Cambridge University Press, 1990). For the Islamic translation movement, see especially Dimitri Gutas, *Greek Thought, Arabic Culture: The Graeco-Arabic Translation Movement in Baghdad and Early Abbasid Society (2nd-4th/8th-10th Centuries)* (London: Routledge, 1998); and A. I. Sabra, "The Appropriation and Subsequent Naturalization of Greek Science in Medieval Islam: A Preliminary Statement," in F. Jamil Ragep and Sally P. Ragep with Steven Livesey, eds. *Tradition, Transmission, Transformation: Proceedings of Two Conferences on Pre-Modern Science Held at the University of Oklahoma* (Leiden: E. J. Brill, 1996): 3-27. Jonathan M. Bloom's *Paper before Print: The History and Impact of Paper in the Islamic World* (New Haven, Conn.: Yale University Press, 2001) is a superb study which embraces a capacious range of subjects beyond paper per se, including books, art, and various forms of notation including mathematical notation. An older but still useful book is David Diringer, *The Book Before Printing: Ancient, Medieval and Oriental* (1953; reprint, New York: Dover Publications, 1982). A series of small books associated in one way or another with the British Library provide welcome technical detail on a variety of topics related to book production: Michelle P. Brown, *Understanding Illuminated Manuscripts: A Guide to Technical Terms* (Malibu, Calif.: J. Paul Getty Museum and British Library, 1994); Michelle P. Brown, *The British Library Guide to Writing and Scripts: History and Techniques* (London: The

143

British Library, 1998); P. J. M. Marks, *The British Library Guide to Bookbinding: History and Techniques* (London: The British Library, 1998); and Christopher de Hamel, *The British Library Guide to Manuscript Illumination: History and Techniques* (London: The British Library, 2001). For the codex, see Colin H. Roberts and T. C. Skeat, *The Birth of the Codex* (Oxford: The British Academy and Oxford University Press, 1983). And see Duncan Haldane, *Islamic Bookbindings in the Victoria and Albert Museum* (London: World of Islam Festival Trust and the Victoria and Albert Museum, 1983); and Johannes Pedersen, *The Arabic Book*, trans. Geoffrey French, ed. Robert Hillenbrand (Princeton, N.J.: Princeton University Press, 1984).